BIOGRAPHIES *of the* CIVIL WAR AND RECONSTRUCTION

ABRAHAM LINCOLN, ROBERT E. LEE, ULYSSES S. GRANT, AND MORE

IMPACT ON AMERICA: COLLECTIVE BIOGRAPHIES

BIOGRAPHIES of the CIVIL WAR AND RECONSTRUCTION

ABRAHAM LINCOLN, ROBERT E. LEE, ULYSSES S. GRANT, AND MORE

Edited by Sherman Hollar

Britannica Educational Publishing
IN ASSOCIATION WITH
ROSEN
EDUCATIONAL SERVICES

Published in 2013 by Britannica Educational Publishing
(a trademark of Encyclopædia Britannica, Inc.)
in association with Rosen Educational Services, LLC
29 East 21st Street, New York, NY 10010.

Distributed exclusively by Rosen Educational Services.
For a listing of additional Britannica Educational Publishing titles, call toll free (800) 237-9932.

First Edition

Britannica Educational Publishing
J.E. Luebering: Director, Core Reference Group, Encyclopædia Britannica
Adam Augustyn: Assistant Manager, Encyclopædia Britannica

Anthony L. Green: Editor, Compton's by Britannica
Michael Anderson: Senior Editor, Compton's by Britannica
Andrea R. Field: Senior Editor, Compton's by Britannica
Sherman Hollar: Senior Editor, Compton's by Britannica

Marilyn L. Barton: Senior Coordinator, Production Control
Steven Bosco: Director, Editorial Technologies
Lisa S. Braucher: Senior Producer and Data Editor
Yvette Charboneau: Senior Copy Editor
Kathy Nakamura: Manager, Media Acquisition

Rosen Educational Services
Hope Lourie Killcoyne: Executive Editor
Nelson Sá: Art Director
Cindy Reiman: Photography Manager
Karen Huang: Photo Researcher
Brian Garvey: Designer, Cover Design
Introduction by Hope Lourie Killcoyne

Library of Congress Cataloging-in-Publication Data

Biographies of the Civil War and Reconstruction: Abraham Lincoln, Robert E. Lee, Ulysses S. Grant, and more/edited by Sherman Hollar.—1st ed.
p. cm.—(Impact on America--collective biographies)
"In association with Britannica Educational Publishing, Rosen Educational Services."
Includes bibliographical references and index.
ISBN 978-1-61530-692-3 (library binding)
1. United States—History—Civil War, 1861–1865—Biography. 2. Reconstruction (U.S. history, 1865–1877)—Biography. I. Hollar, Sherman.
E467.B565 2013
973.7092'2—dc23
[B]

2012001380

Manufactured in the United States of America

Cover, p. 3 blewisphotography/Shutterstock.com (reins, gun), © iStockphoto.com/DNY59 (cap), Library of Congress Prints and Photographs Division, Washington, D.C. (Abraham Lincoln, Ulysses S. Grant); back cover © www.istockphoto.com/Sodafish bvba; interior background images © www.istockphoto.com/oliopi (geometric), © www.istockphoto.com/Bill Noll (floral)

CONTENTS

Introduction 8

Ch. 1 Millard Fillmore 12
Ch. 2 Franklin Pierce 17
Ch. 3 James Buchanan. 21
Ch. 4 Dred Scott 26
Ch. 5 Thaddeus Stevens 28
Ch. 6 Sojourner Truth 30
Ch. 7 John Brown 33
Ch. 8 David Farragut 38
Ch. 9 Robert E. Lee 40
Ch. 10 Joseph E. Johnston 45
Ch. 11 Jefferson Davis 48
Ch. 12 Abraham Lincoln 53
Ch. 13 Andrew Johnson 64
Ch. 14 Harriet Beecher Stowe. 69
Ch. 15 Horace Greeley 73
Ch. 16 Wendell Phillips 75
Ch. 17 Stephen A. Douglas 78
Ch. 18 George G. Meade 80

Ch. 19 Jubal A. Early 82
Ch. 20 Benjamin F. Butler 86
Ch. 21 Julia Ward Howe 89
Ch. 22 William Tecumseh Sherman . 91
Ch. 23 Harriet Tubman 97
Ch. 24 James Longstreet 102
Ch. 25 Nathan Bedford Forrest . . 104
Ch. 26 Clara Barton 107
Ch. 27 Ulysses S. Grant 110
Ch. 28 Hiram R. Revels 118
Ch. 29 Mathew brady 120
Ch. 30 Mary Chesnut 124
Ch. 31 Stonewall Jackson 126
Ch. 32 Winfield Scott Hancock . . 130
Ch. 33 George B. McClellan 132
Ch. 34 Philip Sheridan 136
Ch. 35 Petroleum V. Nasby 140
Ch. 36 Jeb Stuart 142
Ch. 37 John Wilkes Booth 145

CH. 38 ROBERT SMALLS 147
CH. 39 SARAH EDMONDS 149

CONCLUSION 151
GLOSSARY 153
FOR MORE INFORMATION 157
FOR FURTHER READING 160
INDEX 161

INTRODUCTION

During the American Civil War, where you lived—North or South—generally determined which side you were on.

Generally, but not always.

Take legendary naval officer David Farragut, who was born in the South, in a cabin near Knoxville, Tenn. At the time that the Civil War began, the nearly 60-year-old Farragut had a wife and home in Virginia. Nonetheless, Farragut declared his allegiance to the Union. Another native of Tennessee, Andrew Johnson, a U.S. senator who would later become the 17th president of the United States, vehemently opposed secession and was the only Southern senator not to resign his post when the South seceded.

For those soldiers who did fight for the side that their place of birth had dealt them, the beliefs held by said side weren't necessarily held in the fighter's heart. Such was the case with the brilliant Confederate general Robert E. Lee. Although he fought valiantly for the South, Lee believed neither in slavery nor secession. And despite his extraordinary success as a soldier, Lee at

A Currier & Ives lithograph of Confederate General Robert E. Lee, c. 1860 to 1870. Library of Congress, Washington, D.C.

times seemed uneasy with the idea of war itself—for example, when he expressed in a letter to his son before the outbreak of the war his deep dismay at a "union that can only be maintained by swords and bayonets, and in which strife and civil war are to take the place of brotherly love and kindness."

Aside from the issues that led to the war and the rationales of the soldiers involved in the conflict, readers of this book will also learn quite a bit about the presidents of the time and their lives before taking office. Included within are interesting details such as which president once sold real estate, which was a tailor, which had his name changed because of the 19th-century equivalent of a typo, courtesy of West Point, which one attended school for only a year, and which one did not go to school at all.

But this book goes well beyond the lives of the presidents who served in this era. Readers will also learn about the famous Confederate general who, seriously wounded in battle, died soon thereafter as a result of friendly fire, and about the life of the well-known Union general who, much to President Abraham Lincoln's consternation, was clearly reluctant to go into battle.

Looking back on historical events can have a way of making them seem inevitable. When it comes to the Civil War and its aftermath, we all know that slavery ended, that the North won, and that the country moved forward as a single nation, albeit one that faced grave problems of readjustment and reconstruction. But reading about those who peopled the era—whether brave or brilliant, villainous or vanquished—makes the events, the decisions, and the mistakes come alive. In addition, going beyond the famous to introduce lesser-known figures, such as the Northern woman who disguised herself as a man, signed up as a volunteer, and participated in several key battles, adds dimension to a story that still surprises, educates, and unfolds.

All that and more awaits in this volume that chronicles the lives of the 19th-century men and women whose beliefs, actions, and legacies changed the course of American history—all during a time in which the end of slavery and the future direction of the country were anything but certain.

CHAPTER 1

MILLARD FILLMORE

In 1850 the United States was close to civil war over the seemingly impassable problems of slavery. A proposed compromise had touched off the greatest political storm in the nation's history. Amid this bitter struggle President Zachary Taylor suddenly died on July 9, 1850. Succeeding to the presidency was Vice President Millard Fillmore, a Whig from New York. Fillmore worked hard to secure the passage of five separate measures dealing with the slavery problem. This set of laws, called the Compromise of 1850, postponed war for another ten years. It also ended Fillmore's political career. The Whig party refused to nominate him for a second term in 1852, and Fillmore thus became the nation's last Whig president.

Fillmore was born in a log cabin on a frontier farm in Cayuga County, N.Y., on Jan. 7, 1800. Work on the farm took up most of young Millard's time and he was unable to attend school more than three months each year. When he was 14 years old his father hired Millard out for seven years as a

Millard Fillmore. Library of Congress, Washington, D.C.

woolworker. After five years the boy secured his release for $30. He went to Buffalo where he worked in a law office for room and board. He studied law and was admitted to the bar in 1823. In 1826 he married Abigail Powers of Moravia, N.Y. They reared two children, Mary Abigail and Millard Powers.

In 1828 Fillmore was elected to the New York legislature. Four years later he was elected to Congress, where he joined the Whig party in opposition to President Andrew Jackson. Except for one term (1835–37) Fillmore served in Congress continously until 1843.

Defeated in a campaign for governor in 1844, Fillmore won election as state comptroller three years later. Meanwhile, supported by Henry Clay of Kentucky, Fillmore had become one of the most prominent Whigs in the party. On the burning question of slavery he followed a moderate course. This made him acceptable to both Northern and Southern Whigs and led to his nomination and election as Zachary Taylor's vice president in 1848.

When President Taylor died, Fillmore became president and immediately formed a new Cabinet with the famous orator Daniel

Webster as secretary of state. Fillmore also gave his full support to the Compromise of 1850 because he felt that this was the only way to preserve the Union. These pieces of legislation, devised by Henry Clay, were designed to settle the slavery issue to the South's satisfaction in the large new territories that had been won in the Mexican War. Under these measures, California was admitted to the Union as a free state, but the question of slavery in the new territories of New Mexico and Utah was left to be settled by the local residents. Without the compromise, civil war was a genuine threat.

Except for this series of measures there was no important legislation passed during Fillmore's term. Like the other presidents between Jackson and Abraham Lincoln, Fillmore could not win a second term. His support of the Compromise of 1850 cost him the backing of many party leaders in the North. The Whig convention of 1852 ignored the president and nominated General Winfield Scott, a national hero of the Mexican War. Scott, however, was defeated by the Democratic candidate, Franklin Pierce. This campaign proved to be the last in which the Whigs took an effective part.

At the next presidential election, in 1856, the dying Whig party formed an alliance with the Know Nothing, or American, party. They made Fillmore their candidate for president. He carried only one state (Maryland), running far behind Democrat James Buchanan and John C. Frémont, the first presidential nominee of the new Republican party.

Fillmore retired to Buffalo, where he became a leader in the city's civic and cultural life. In 1858, some five years after the death of his wife Abigail, he married Caroline Carmichael McIntosh, from Albany. Fillmore continued to take an active interest in public affairs. He opposed Lincoln's conduct of the Civil War and supported General George B. McClellan for president in the 1864 election. After the war, he sided with the Reconstruction policies of President Andrew Johnson. Fillmore died in Buffalo on March 8, 1874.

CHAPTER 2

FRANKLIN PIERCE

In 1852 the Democrats could not agree on one of their party leaders for a presidential nomination. They finally turned to a little-known New Hampshire lawyer, Franklin Pierce, as their candidate.

At the time of Pierce's election the slavery issue had been temporarily quieted by the Compromise of 1850. When the problem suddenly recurred during his administration, Pierce had little success in dealing with it. His shifting views made him unpopular, especially in the North, and he failed to win a second term.

Pierce was born on a frontier farm in Hillsboro, N.H., on Nov. 23, 1804. His father, Benjamin Pierce, served 13 years in the New Hampshire state legislature and two terms as governor of that state. During his youth the future president attended private schools. He graduated from Bowdoin College in 1824. After studying law for three years he was admitted to the bar. In 1829, the same year his father won his second term as governor, Pierce was elected to the New Hampshire

Franklin Pierce. Library of Congress, Washington, D.C.

state legislature. He served four years in this office, and in 1831–32 he was named speaker of the lower house.

At the age of 29 Pierce was elected to Congress. A supporter of President Andrew Jackson's policies, Pierce was sent to the Senate in 1837, the youngest senator at that time. Pierce resigned from the Senate in 1842 to practice law in Concord, N.H. When the Mexican War broke out he enlisted in the Army as a private. Soon commissioned as a brigadier general, he served under General Winfield Scott in the campaign against Mexico City. Pierce resigned from the Army after the war.

When the Democratic national convention met in 1852 there were so many strong candidates for the presidential nomination that none could win the required two-thirds vote. To break the deadlock the convention finally nominated Pierce on the 49th ballot. William R. King of Alabama was the candidate for vice president. Opposing Pierce was the Whig nominee, General Scott. Pierce carried all but four of the 31 states, receiving an electoral vote of 254 to Scott's 42.

During his administration Pierce angered many Democrats by urging passage of the

Kansas-Nebraska Act, providing popular sovereignty in those territories. This measure reopened the slavery problem and spurred formation of the antislavery Republican party.

Pierce sought his party's renomination for president in 1856, but the Democrats nominated James Buchanan instead. When his term ended, Pierce returned to New Hampshire to practice law. He died on Oct. 8, 1869, in Concord.

CHAPTER 3

JAMES BUCHANAN

When James Buchanan became president in 1857 he had a record of 42 years of almost continuous public service. Even with this long experience, he was not a successful leader in a time of great crisis for the United States.

The problems of slavery had gradually divided the nation into two hostile parts—the North and the South. As his term was ending, seven slave states of the deep South used the event of Abraham Lincoln's election to secede from the Union. They set up an independent government, the Confederate States of America. Buchanan was unable to prevent this action. The result was the American Civil War.

Buchanan was born near Mercersburg, Pa., on April 23, 1791. At the age of 16 he entered Dickinson College. After his graduation he studied law in Lancaster. He was admitted to the bar in 1812. After working as a lawyer for two years Buchanan entered politics, winning election to the Pennsylvania House of Representatives for the first of two terms.

In 1820 Buchanan was elected to the U.S. House of Representatives. Here he served ten years. He became minister to Russia in 1832 and negotiated the first commercial treaty with that country for the United States. Two years later he was elected to the U.S. Senate. Twice reelected, he served until 1845 when he resigned to become secretary of state under President James Knox Polk.

At the end of Polk's administration, Buchanan retired to his newly purchased estate, Wheatland, near Lancaster, Pa. He was a strong candidate for the Democratic nomination for president in 1852 but lost to Franklin Pierce. He supported Pierce in the campaign and was named minister to Great Britain.

At the Democratic convention of 1856 Buchanan was unanimously nominated for president on the 17th ballot. John C. Breckinridge of Kentucky was nominated for vice president. Opposing Buchanan was the Republican party's first presidential candidate, John Charles Frémont. Former president Millard Fillmore was the nominee of both the American (Know Nothing) and Whig parties.

Although they received fewer than half of the popular votes cast, "Buck and Breck" were elected with a total of 174 electoral votes; Frémont received 114; Fillmore, 8. Buchanan carried every slaveholding state except Maryland, which went to Fillmore.

As president, Buchanan could find no way to deal effectively with the critical question of slavery. The split between the slave and the free states steadily widened, and the danger of secession became ever greater. There was hope that the problem might be settled by a court decision. This hope faded when almost the entire North rejected the 1857 verdict of the Supreme Court in the Dred Scott case. This ruling made slavery legal in all U.S. territories. (Read the next chapter for more on the controversial decision.)

Civil war was already raging in Kansas, where slaveholders and Free-Soilers (members of a political party opposed to the extension of slavery into the territories) tried to gain control of the state government. Influenced by threats of secession from radical Southerners, Buchanan urged Congress to admit Kansas as a state under the 1858 Lecompton Constitution. This would have permitted slavery in the state. Congress refused to accept the constitution, and Kansas was kept out of the Union for another three years.

In 1860 the Democratic party split into two groups. Neither of the groups would accept Buchanan as its nominee, because it was obvious he could not win. The Northern Democrats named Stephen A. Douglas for president; the Southern Democrats chose Vice President Breckinridge. This split secured the election of Republican candidate Abraham Lincoln.

Buchanan's administration reached a crisis during the winter of 1860–61, between the election and the inauguration of Lincoln. The victory of a Republican president opposed to the extension of slavery led to actual secession by Southern states. On Dec. 20, 1860, South Carolina withdrew from the Union. By Feb. 1, 1861, Mississippi, Florida, Alabama, Georgia, and Louisiana had seceded, and on March 2 Texas joined the Confederacy.

Although he opposed secession, Buchanan believed that there was no way for him to prevent such action. In January 1861 he sent the steamer *Star of the West* to resupply besieged Fort Sumter in South Carolina. When the ship was turned back by the Confederates, Buchanan abandoned all attempts to assist Federal outposts in the South. Meanwhile the Union's war supplies in the South were lost.

When Buchanan retired in March 1861, he was under attack from critics in both the North and South. Although he upheld President Lincoln's policies during the Civil War, he claimed that as president he could not have acted other than as he did. In 1866 he published a defense of his actions entitled *Mr. Buchanan's Administration on the Eve of the Rebellion*. Buchanan died on June 1, 1868, and was buried in Lancaster, Pa.

CHAPTER 4

DRED SCOTT

The controversial 1857 ruling of the U.S. Supreme Court in the case of Dred Scott made slavery legal in all the territories. Dred Scott was a black slave who was owned by Dr. John Emerson of Missouri. In 1834 Emerson began a series of moves as part of his service in the U.S. military. He took Scott from Missouri (a slave state) to Illinois (a free state) and finally into the Wisconsin Territory (a free territory under the provisions of the Missouri Compromise). During this period, Scott met and married Harriet Robinson, who became part of the Emerson household. In the early 1840s the Emersons (Dr. Emerson had married in 1838) and the Scotts returned to Missouri. Emerson died in 1843.

Dred Scott reportedly attempted to purchase his freedom from Emerson's widow, who refused the sale. In 1846, with the help of antislavery lawyers, Harriet and Dred Scott filed individual lawsuits for their freedom in Missouri on the grounds that their residence in a free state and a free territory had freed them from the bonds of slavery. It was later agreed that only Dred's case would move forward; the decision in that case would apply to Harriet's case as well.

The case was carried to the U.S. Supreme Court. On March 6, 1857, a majority of the court (seven out of nine), through the opinion of Chief Justice Roger B. Taney, declared that Scott was still a slave and not a citizen and so had no constitutional right to sue in a federal court. The decision further held that Congress had no power to prohibit slavery in the territories and that the Missouri Compromise therefore was unconstitutional.

President James Buchanan urged all the people to accept the decision as final, but antislavery leaders in the North continued their agitation against slavery. By convincing many Northerners that Southern slaveholders were determined to rule the nation, the Dred Scott decision served to widen the gap between the North and the South and helped bring on the American Civil War.

The Scotts were later bought by the Blow family, who had sold Dred to Emerson, and they were freed in 1857. Dred Scott died of tuberculosis the following year. Little is known of Harriet Scott's life after that time.

CHAPTER 5

THADDEUS STEVENS

An influential legislator during the American Civil War and the Reconstruction period that followed, Thaddeus Stevens fought to end slavery and to win citizenship for the former slaves.

Stevens was born on April 4, 1792, near Danville, Vt. He studied at Dartmouth College and from 1816 practiced law in Pennsylvania, often defending fugitive slaves without fee. In the U.S. House of Representatives, where he served from 1849 to 1853 as a Whig, he opposed the fugitive-slave provision of the Compromise of 1850. This provision required the federal government to aid in the capture and return of runaway slaves to their former owners. In 1858 Stevens was elected as a Republican to Congress, where he became a recognized leader who opposed the extension of slavery into the Western territories. He led the Radicals—the majority Republican faction—in advocating emancipation.

After the war Stevens denounced President Andrew Johnson for readmitting some former Confederate states to the

Union, arguing that they had committed treason and should be made territories until they wrote constitutions that provided for black suffrage. He demanded that rebel property be confiscated and divided into homesteads for blacks. He also helped formulate the 14th Amendment to the Constitution, which conferred citizenship on the former slaves. The disputes between Congress and President Johnson led Stevens to introduce the resolution for the president's impeachment in 1868. Stevens died on Aug. 11, 1868, in Washington, D.C.

CHAPTER 6

SOJOURNER TRUTH

"Children, I talk to God and God talks to me!" This was the usual opening of abolitionist, or antislavery, speaker and civil rights pioneer Sojourner Truth. Her real name was Isabella Van Wagener, and she was born a slave in Ulster County, N.Y., in about 1797.

The circumstances surrounding her liberation are uncertain, but her surname was taken from Isaac Van Wagener, who was reportedly the last of several masters and the man who freed her in 1827. She moved to New York City, where she worked as a domestic servant. There she became closely associated with a Christian evangelist named Elijah Pierson. In 1843 she left New York, took the name Sojourner Truth, and began a life of preaching that carried her throughout the Northern states. Her growing reputation and personal magnetism drew large crowds wherever she appeared. She supported herself by selling copies of

Sojourner Truth. Hulton Archive/Getty Images

The Narrative of Sojourner Truth, which she had dictated to a friend.

Sojourner Truth was a powerful foe of slavery, and in the 1850s she added the women's rights movement to her causes. During the Civil War Truth served as a counselor to freed slaves in Washington, D.C. Her later years were spent helping freed slaves and lecturing in the North. She died at her home in Battle Creek, Mich., on Nov. 26, 1883.

CHAPTER 7

JOHN BROWN

The ideological differences between the North and the South that festered before the American Civil War were reflected in their views of the abolitionist John Brown. To Northerners he was a martyr to the cause of freeing African Americans from slavery. To Southerners he was an insane criminal. As for historians, he was a man obsessed who chose a lawless course in order to achieve a moral end. Brown regarded himself as an instrument of God.

John Brown was born on May 9, 1800, in Torrington, Conn. His father was a tanner, shoemaker, and farmer who had 16 children by three wives. The family moved to Ohio in 1805. As a young man, Brown followed his father's trades, sold wool, and tried surveying. At 20 he married Dianthe Lusk. They had seven children. In 1833, a year after Lusk died, he married Mary Anne Day. They had 13 children. Brown was barely able to support his family as they moved about in Ohio, Pennsylvania, Massachusetts, and New York.

The son of a staunch abolitionist, Brown was convinced that black slavery was a sin against Christianity. In Pennsylvania his home was a station on the Underground Railroad, a secret network to aid fugitive slaves. In New York he settled his family in a black community founded on land donated by an antislavery philanthropist. By the time he was in his 50s, Brown had finally decided that force was the only way left to banish slavery.

In 1854 several of Brown's sons settled at Osawatomie, in Kansas Territory. Brown joined them in the bloody fights to make Kansas a free state. (One son was killed in a skirmish.) In May 1856 Brown led a small band of men who sought revenge for murders by proslavery mobs and brutally killed five settlers suspected of proslavery beliefs. He became feared as "Old Osawatomie Brown," a ruthless guerrilla leader pitted against the slaveholders. When the Kansas question was settled in favor of freedom, Brown schemed for a slave insurrection in the South itself.

On a rented farm in Maryland Brown gathered an armed band of 16 whites and five blacks to attack the federal arsenal

John Brown, flag in hand, taking an oath c. 1856. Fotosearch/ Archive Photos/Getty Images

across the Potomac River at Harpers Ferry (now in West Virginia) on the night of Oct. 16, 1859. He wanted weapons for an "army of emancipation" to liberate other slaves. They took 60 hostages and held out against the local militia but finally surrendered to U.S. Marines under the command of Colonel Robert E. Lee. Ten of Brown's men, including two of his sons, were killed. Brown was among those wounded and taken prisoner.

Convicted by the Commonwealth of Virginia of treason, murder, and inciting slaves to rebellion, Brown was hanged on Dec. 2, 1859. At his trial he declared "[I would] forfeit my life for the furtherance of the ends of justice, and mingle my blood further with the blood of my children and with the blood of millions in this slave country whose rights are disregarded by wicked, cruel, and unjust enactments..."

African Americans revered Brown for his long dedication to their welfare. As early as 1847 the great black abolitionist Frederick Douglass described Brown as a man who was "in sympathy a black man, and as deeply interested in our cause, as though his own soul had been pierced with the iron of slavery."

After the raid on Harpers Ferry, Southerners feared that other Northern radicals would follow Brown's violent example. Many Northerners who had been indifferent to slavery became convinced that abolition was necessary. Historians now believe that Brown's action helped bring on the Civil War. Once the war had begun, Brown was immortalized in a song in which his soul went "marching on."

CHAPTER 8

DAVID FARRAGUT

The ranks of rear admiral, vice-admiral, and admiral of the U.S. Navy were created successively to reward the services and acknowledge the genius of David Farragut. His captures of New Orleans and Mobile Bay in the Civil War find parallels only in Horatio Nelson's victories of Copenhagen, the Nile, and Trafalgar.

David Glasgow Farragut was born on July 5, 1801, in a cabin near Knoxville, Tenn. His mother died when he was seven, and Farragut was adopted by Commodore David Porter, a family friend. Porter secured an appointment as midshipman for the boy before his tenth birthday. The U.S. Naval Academy was not established until 1845, so cadets were educated and trained at sea.

In the War of 1812 Midshipman Farragut sailed on the *Essex* to the South Pacific. He took a captured British ship into Santiago, Chile, at the age of 12 and conducted himself with coolness and courage in the bloody defeat of the *Essex* by two British ships. Forty-five years of routine duty followed.

When the Civil War came, Farragut was a captain and nearly 60. Although a Southerner by birth, with a wife and home in Virginia, he decided that his allegiance belonged to the Union. He was given command of a superb fleet of heavy ships, gunboats, and mortar boats and was ordered to open the mouth of the Mississippi River by taking New Orleans. The way up the river was defended by two forts, between which stretched a heavy iron chain. Farragut broke the chain, ran his fleet past the forts, evaded a fire ship, sank the defense fleet, and in April 1862 captured New Orleans.

For 16 months more he saw service on the Mississippi, aiding materially in the taking of Vicksburg. Then he was ordered to take Mobile Bay, the last Confederate stronghold on the Gulf of Mexico. The entrance to the bay was guarded by Forts Gaines and Morgan; the channel was filled with mines—then known as torpedoes. "Damn the torpedoes!" Farragut shouted, and ordered his fleet ahead. All but one of his 18 ships passed safely by. Fort Gaines fell two days later, on Aug. 7, 1864; Fort Morgan was finally taken on August 23.

After this battle he retired from active duty and settled in New York City. For his six remaining years he enjoyed honors such as have been accorded few Americans. Farragut died on Aug. 14, 1870.

CHAPTER 9

ROBERT E. LEE

The Confederacy's greatest soldier, Robert E. Lee, was descended from an old and honored family. Several of Lee's forebears had played distinguished roles in Virginia's history. His father was the Revolutionary War hero Light-Horse Harry Lee, a friend of George Washington.

The family was living at Stratford, Va., the ancestral home in Westmoreland County, when Robert was born on Jan. 19, 1807. Partly because of the military tradition in his family and partly because an army career was attractive to him, young Lee decided to become a soldier. He graduated from West Point in 1829. On July 5, 1831, he married Mary Custis, great-granddaughter of Washington's wife, Martha. The Lees had seven children.

Lee's first experience in battle came in the Mexican War. He was one of a group of young engineer officers on the staff of General Winfield Scott, the general in chief of the army. Lee was the ablest of the engineer officers and served with distinction in all the operations of Scott's victorious campaign.

Robert E. Lee, photographed by Mathew Brady, April 16, 1865.
Mathew Brady/Archive Photos/Getty Images

After the Mexican War, Lee's next big assignment was as superintendent of West Point. From there, he went to Texas in 1855 as lieutenant colonel of the Second Cavalry Regiment. In 1859 he was home on leave when the abolitionist John Brown tried to start a slave uprising at Harpers Ferry in Virginia. Lee led a party of Marines that captured Brown and his band. In 1861 Lee was offered command of a new army being formed to force the seceded Southern states back into the Union. Though opposed to secession, he refused. After Virginia voted to secede, Lee resigned from the Army to offer his services to the "defense of [his] native state."

In June 1862 Jefferson Davis, president of the Confederacy, appointed Lee commander of the organization that was known as the Army of Northern Virginia. In the ensuing Seven Days' Battles that took place in June and July around the city of Richmond, Va., Lee drove the Union Army back about 25 miles (40 kilometers) but was not able to destroy it. In August he inflicted another decisive defeat on the North at the Second Battle of Bull Run, forcing the Federal troops to retreat from northern Virginia all the way back to Washington.

Lee next decided to invade Maryland. The commander of the Union forces, General

George B. McClellan, moved to meet him. The two met in September at the Battle of Antietam, where McClellan attacked Lee but failed to break his lines. Lee, realizing that he was in a dangerous position and far from his supplies, retreated and took up a defensive position behind the Rappahannock River in northern Virginia. Here General Ambrose E. Burnside, who succeeded McClellan, attacked Lee in December at the Battle of Fredericksburg and met a bloody repulse. As the year 1862 closed, Lee had given the Confederacy its greatest victories and had become the idol of the Southern people.

After the Battle of Chancellorsville in May 1863, in which Lee had achieved victory by splitting up his army and encircling the opposing forces in one of the most audacious moves in military history, he started an offensive movement he hoped would win the war—an invasion of Pennsylvania. In the southern part of that state, he met the defending Federal Army at Gettysburg in a three-day battle, from July 1 to 3, the greatest ever fought in North America. On the second and third days Lee threw strong attacks against the Union lines but was repulsed with heavy losses.

After Gettysburg, Lee fell back into northern Virginia. For the rest of the war, with his army getting ever smaller, he had to employ a defensive strategy. In the spring of 1864, General Ulysses S. Grant assumed direction of the Federal Army in Virginia. His objective was to bring Lee to battle and to destroy the Confederate Army. Lee evaded attempts to trap him into decisive battle and inflicted heavy losses on Grant at the battles of the Wilderness, Spotsylvania, and Cold Harbor.

In the spring of 1865, after Grant had seized the railroads that carried supplies to Lee's army, Lee was forced to abandon Petersburg and Richmond. He retreated to the west, but Grant was right on his heels. With only 25,000 men left, Lee realized that his cause was hopeless. To continue fighting meant the needless loss of lives. Early in April he met Grant at Appomattox and surrendered the Army of Northern Virginia.

In the years after the war, Lee was the hero of the South. With dignity and without bitterness, he accepted defeat and preached to his people the necessity of peace and national unity. Offered many jobs, he accepted the presidency of Washington College at Lexington, Va. Later it became Washington and Lee University. He died in Lexington on Oct. 12, 1870.

CHAPTER 10

JOSEPH E. JOHNSTON

One of the Confederacy's most effective officers, Joseph E. Johnston never suffered a direct defeat during the American Civil War. His military effectiveness, though, was hindered by a long-standing feud with the president of the Confederacy, Jefferson Davis.

Johnston was born on Feb. 3, 1807, near Farmville, Va. A graduate of West Point, he resigned his commission at the outbreak of the Civil War to offer his services to his native state of Virginia. Given the rank of brigadier general in the Confederate Army of the Shenandoah, he was credited in July 1861 with the first important Southern victory at the First Battle of Bull Run. He was promoted to general and defended Richmond during the Peninsular Campaign of 1862. Although objecting to the strategy prescribed by Davis, he fought well against the Union forces. Severely wounded at the Battle of Fair Oaks in May, he was replaced by General Robert E. Lee.

A year later Johnston assumed control of Confederate forces in Mississippi threatened by the Federal advance on Vicksburg. He warned General John C. Pemberton to evacuate the city, but President Davis counterordered Pemberton to hold it at all costs. Lacking sufficient troops, Johnston could not relieve Pemberton, and Vicksburg fell on July 4, 1863. Bitterly criticized, Johnston nonetheless took command of the Army of the Tennessee in December as the combined armies of the North advanced toward Atlanta, Ga. Subsequent events demonstrated the soundness of Johnston's strategy of planned withdrawal to avoid a defeat by superior forces and the disintegration of the Confederate Army; nevertheless, Davis, dissatisfied with Johnston's failure to defeat the invaders, replaced him in July.

Restored to duty in February 1865, Johnston took command of his old army, now in North Carolina, and succeeded in delaying the advance of General William T. Sherman at Bentonville, in March. But lack of men and supplies forced Johnston to order continued withdrawal, and he surrendered to Sherman at Durham Station, N.C., on April 26.

After the war, Johnston engaged in business ventures, wrote his memoirs, served in the U.S. House of Representatives (1879–81), and was named U.S. commissioner of railroads in 1885. He died on March 21, 1891, in Washington, D.C.

CHAPTER 11

JEFFERSON DAVIS

During the American Civil War, Jefferson Davis was president of the Confederate States of America. A hero of the Mexican War and former U.S. war secretary, he also took an active role in dictating Confederate military strategy during the Civil War.

Both Davis and his eventual adversary, Abraham Lincoln, were born in Kentucky. Davis was born on June 3, 1808, in what is now Fairview, the 10th child of farmers. The family soon moved to a small plantation in Mississippi. His parents were not wealthy, but his oldest brother, Joseph, became well-to-do and helped him. Davis attended academies in Kentucky and Mississippi, and in 1821 he entered Transylvania University in Kentucky. Three years later he was appointed to West Point. He graduated in 1828, becoming an officer in the U.S. Army. He served in frontier posts in Illinois and Wisconsin and in the Black Hawk War in 1832.

In 1835 Davis resigned his commission and returned to Mississippi and ran a plantation. He was elected to Congress in 1845,

Jefferson Davis. **Library of Congress Prints and Photographs Division**

but he resigned the next year when the Mexican War broke out. He became a colonel of Mississippi volunteers. At the Battle of Buena Vista, Davis and his regiment probably saved the U.S. Army from defeat. Davis, who was severely wounded in the battle, became widely known as "the hero of Buena Vista."

In 1847 Mississippi sent Davis to the U.S. Senate. His ability as a speaker and his call for the extension of slavery into the Western territories made him a leader among Southern Democrats. In 1851 he resigned and ran for governor of Mississippi. He was defeated, but he reentered public life in 1853 when President Franklin Pierce made him secretary of war. Davis served until the end of Pierce's term in 1857.

Mississippi again sent him to the Senate. By this time the tension between the North and the South over slavery was at fever heat. Davis took an unyielding attitude in favor of slavery. In 1860 he helped nominate a proslavery Democrat to run for president against both the Northern Democratic nominee and the Republican nominee, Abraham Lincoln. This party split helped Lincoln to be elected.

At first Davis did not want the Southern states to secede, or withdraw, from the

Union, though he believed it was their constitutional right to do so. He spoke throughout many parts of the country urging cooperation between North and South.

Mississippi was the second state to secede, however, in early 1861. Soon after, on Jan. 21, 1861, Davis made an impassioned speech to the Senate and resigned. Almost immediately he was made commander of Mississippi's armed forces. Within a couple of weeks he was named president of the Confederacy. Despite poor health, he was inaugurated on Feb. 18, 1861. His first act was to dispatch peace delegates to the United States, but Lincoln would not receive them. The war soon began.

Davis formed a strong central government. At first his administration was highly popular, and his armed forces successful. But his brand-new government faced considerable problems: the Confederacy was seriously outnumbered and undersupplied, it had few manufacturing plants or railroads, and it was wracked by internal political disputes. As the war progressed, time brought military reverses, and criticism began.

In April 1865 General Robert E. Lee, commander of the Confederate forces, surrendered without Davis' approval. Davis moved his cabinet south, but he soon was captured by U.S. troops near Irwinville, Ga.

Davis was confined at Fort Monroe. Indicted for treason but never tried, he was released on bail in 1867, and the case against him was later dropped. His U.S. citizenship was posthumously reinstated in 1978.

As soon as he was free he journeyed to Canada and Europe to try to regain his health. Upon his return he tried to mend his broken fortunes. His business ventures proved failures, however, and in 1878 he retired. The rest of his life was spent writing his book *The Rise and Fall of the Confederate Government*. He died in New Orleans, La., on Dec. 6, 1889. His body was later moved to Richmond, Va., which had been the capital of the Confederacy.

CHAPTER 12

ABRAHAM LINCOLN

The 16th president of the United States, Abraham Lincoln ranks among the greatest of all American statesmen. When he took office in 1861, the country was at the brink of civil war. During this difficult time Lincoln was firm in his determination to hold the Union together. Along the way he helped bring about the end of slavery in the United States, earning the title of the Great Emancipator. His relevance has endured especially because of the passion with which he championed democracy.

Early Life

Lincoln was born on Feb. 12, 1809, in a one-room log cabin near Hodgenville, Ky. His parents, Thomas and Nancy Hanks Lincoln, were pioneer farmers. When Abe was two years old the family moved to a nearby farm on Knob Creek. Like all farm boys in those days, he learned to plant, hoe, husk corn, build fires, and chop wood. In 1816 the Lincolns moved to southwestern Indiana, settling on

Abraham Lincoln. Library of Congress, Washington, D.C.

Little Pigeon Creek in Spencer County. Abe helped his father build a log cabin and take care of the family's crops.

After Abe's mother died in 1818, Thomas married a widow, Sarah Bush Johnston. She encouraged Abraham's desire to learn. She also made Thomas send the 11-year-old to school. In all, the boy attended school for less than a year, but he made up for it by reading. When he was 15 years old Abe often worked as a hired hand on other farms. Usually, while he plowed or split fence rails, he carried a borrowed book to read while he lunched or rested.

Life in Illinois

In 1830 the Lincoln family moved to Illinois. At the age of 21, Lincoln was about to begin life on his own. Having no desire to be a farmer, he tried his hand at a variety of occupations. As a rail-splitter, he helped to clear and fence his father's new farm. As a flatboatman, he made a voyage down the Mississippi River to New Orleans, La.

Upon his return to Illinois he settled in New Salem, a village of about 25 families on the Sangamon River, about 20 miles (32 kilometers) northwest of Springfield. There he worked from time to time as storekeeper, postmaster, and surveyor. When the Black Hawk War broke out in 1832, Lincoln enlisted as a volunteer and served three months.

Meanwhile, aspiring to be a legislator, Lincoln was defeated in his first bid for the Illinois General Assembly. He won a seat in 1834, however, and was reelected in 1836, 1838, and 1840. By the time he started his second term he was a skilled politician and a leader of the Whig party in Illinois. Encouraged by friends in the legislature, Lincoln decided to become a lawyer. Between terms he borrowed law books to study. In 1836 he received his law license.

In 1837 Lincoln moved his practice from New Salem to Springfield, Ill. He became a successful circuit-riding lawyer, noted for his shrewdness, common sense, and honesty (earning the nickname "Honest Abe"). In 1842 he married Mary Todd. They had four sons.

National Politics

In 1847 Lincoln was elected as a Whig to the U.S. House of Representatives. In 1856 he joined the Republican party, which nominated him as its candidate in the 1858 Senate

One of the earliest known photographs of Lincoln was taken in Springfield, Ill., in 1846, when he was 37 years old. He did not grow his beard until 1861. Library of Congress, Washington, D.C.

election. In a series of seven debates with U.S. Senator Stephen A. Douglas, he argued against the extension of slavery into the territories. Though morally opposed to slavery, he was not an abolitionist; indeed, he attempted to rebut Douglas's charge that he was a dangerous radical by reassuring audiences that he did not favor political equality for blacks. Despite his loss in the election, the debates brought Lincoln national attention.

This photograph was taken in Springfield during Lincoln's "stay-at-home" presidential campaign in 1860. He bought the house in 1843, for 1,500 dollars, then added the second story. **Encyclopædia Britannica Inc.**

In the 1860 presidential election, Lincoln was the Republican candidate. The Democratic party was split, with the North nominating Douglas and the South choosing John C. Breckinridge. Lincoln won the election by a large margin in the electoral college, though he received only two-fifths of the popular vote. He was the first Republican to become president. His vice president was Hannibal Hamlin of Maine.

Alarm spread through the Southern states. They thought a Republican president would not respect their rights or property. They felt that secession was their only hope. Before Lincoln's inauguration seven Southern states seceded from the Union. In his inaugural address Lincoln assured the South that he would respect its rights. Nevertheless, less than six weeks later, on April 12, 1861, the Civil War began.

Presidency

The Civil War completely consumed Lincoln's administration, and he excelled as a wartime leader. When he had trouble finding capable generals early in the war, he read all he could on military science and directed much of the strategy for the Union Army and the Navy himself. He made mistakes, but, on the whole, he was a successful commander in chief. When he found a capable general, such as Ulysses S. Grant, he supported him steadfastly despite great criticism. For the greater part of the war most of the newspapers and people bitterly criticized Lincoln's policies.

Lincoln believed that his primary task in the war was to save the Union. Nevertheless, he knew that the slavery question must be settled if the United States, founded on the principles of liberty and equal rights for all, were to survive as a country. During 1862 Lincoln worked out a plan to free the slaves. On September 22, Lincoln put forth his preliminary proclamation, promising freedom for slaves in any Confederate state that did not return to the Union that year. When the South ignored him, he issued the final Emancipation Proclamation on Jan. 1, 1863. It was a landmark moment that transformed the war from a struggle to preserve the Union into a crusade for human freedom.

In July 1863 the Union armies turned back the Confederate forces at Gettysburg, Pa. On Nov. 19, 1863, the battlefield was dedicated as a national cemetery. The chief speaker was Edward Everett, a noted orator. Lincoln was also invited to speak. He worked and reworked his speech, seeking to make it as perfect as possible. The crowd listened for two hours to Everett's extravagant oratory. Lincoln finished his speech, now called the Gettysburg Address, in a little less than three minutes. The speech honored the Union dead

The Union Christmas Dinner, published in **Harper's Weekly** ***in 1864, depicts President Abraham Lincoln's invitation to the South to rejoin the Union on an equal basis with the other states.*** **Library of Congress, Washington, D.C.**

and the principles of democracy and equality they died for. Everett later wrote to Lincoln: "I should be glad if I could flatter myself that I came as near the central idea of the occasion in two hours as you did in two minutes."

By November 1864 Lincoln was nearly exhausted by the burden of the war and grief at the death of his son Willie in the White House. Wherever he turned he read or heard criticism of himself and his generals. He prepared a memorandum for his Cabinet, forecasting his defeat in the coming election. The people, however, at last rallied to him and reelected him, with Andrew Johnson as vice president. Lincoln's platform had included passage of the 13th Amendment outlawing slavery; the amendment was ratified in 1865. When Lincoln gave his second inaugural address on March 4, 1865, the end of the war was in sight. The president spoke of moderation in reconstructing the South and building a harmonious Union.

Victory and Death

Little more than a month later, on April 9, 1865, Confederate General Robert E. Lee surrendered. To celebrate the end of the war,

Illustration of John Wilkes Booth preparing to assassinate Pres. Abraham Lincoln in the balcony of Ford's Theatre, Washington D.C., April 14, 1865. Kean Collection/Archive Photos/Getty Images

Lincoln took Mary and two guests to Ford's Theatre on the night of April 14. During the play John Wilkes Booth, a young actor who was proslavery and a Confederate sympathizer, crept into the presidential box and shot Lincoln in the head. Early the next morning, on April 15, 1865, Lincoln died. Vice President Johnson assumed the presidency.

CHAPTER 13

ANDREW JOHNSON

Andrew Johnson became a public figure during the Civil War. Although he came from the slave state of Tennessee, Johnson refused to resign as U.S. senator when the state seceded; instead, he worked to preserve the Union. For his efforts he was selected as President Abraham Lincoln's vice presidential running mate in the election of 1864. The two were victorious, and Johnson took office as vice president in March 1865. Six weeks later Lincoln was assassinated and Johnson became president.

In his time Johnson's administration was widely condemned. His reconstruction policies were bitterly opposed in Congress by the Radicals, the majority faction of the Republican party. The resulting political struggles led to an unsuccessful attempt in the Senate to remove him from office

.Johnson was born in Raleigh, N.C., on Dec. 29, 1808. He never attended school, and he taught himself to read and write. After a short apprenticeship as a tailor, he moved with his family to Greeneville, Tenn., where he opened his own tailor shop. Before he was 21 he organized a workingman's party. Elected to the state legislature (1835–43), he became a spokesman for small farmers. He then served in the U.S. House of Representatives (1843–53) and as governor of Tennessee (1853–57).

In 1857 Johnson became a U.S. senator. When secession came in 1860–61, he attracted the attention of the North by his arguments for the Union. People in the North took note of him because he was the only Southern senator who did not resign and side with his state when it seceded. In May 1862 President Lincoln appointed Johnson military governor of Tennessee.

Lincoln and Johnson easily won the 1864 election. Following Lincoln's assassination on April 14, 1865, Johnson faced a series of difficult problems. The Civil War was over but its damages were still to be repaired and the Union restored. The bitterness of the people in the North was increased by the death of Lincoln. Many held the South responsible for this tragedy, and a majority in both houses of Congress were demanding harsh measures against the defeated states.

At first many Congressional leaders liked the idea of Johnson as president. They felt

Campaign poster for the Union nomination with Abraham Lincoln running for president and Andrew Johnson for vice president. The Bridgeman Art Library/Getty Images

that Lincoln would have been too merciful to the South and that Johnson would be more unforgiving. During his early weeks in office the new president seemed to justify this belief. He denounced Confederates as traitors, saying they must be punished and "impoverished."

Soon Johnson changed his attitude. Before Congress met in December 1865 he had recognized state governments in nearly all the seceding states that had not been reconstructed under Lincoln. But Congress refused to seat men from these states, claiming its right to judge the qualifications of prospective Southern members. The remainder of Johnson's administration was dominated by a long and bitter struggle with Congress about the supremacy of legislative over executive rule.

Johnson believed firmly in states' rights. Consequently, he vetoed a bill that would have increased the powers of the Freedmen's Bureau, established as a guardian of the freed slaves. He also vetoed a Civil Rights bill that placed all cases involving the rights of blacks in the federal rather than state courts. Congress passed both of these bills over his veto and then proposed the 14th Amendment to the Constitution. This would deprive the Southern states of their full share of representation in Congress unless they gave blacks the right to vote. It also excluded from office all who had taken part in the rebellion until they were pardoned by a two-thirds vote of each house.

In 1867 and 1868 Congress passed a series of four reconstruction acts establishing military rule and conditions of readmission for ten Southern states. Johnson vetoed every one of these measures, but each time Congress overrode the president's disapproval.

In 1868 the quarrel between Johnson and the Radical Republicans in Congress came to a head. The president sought to remove Edwin M. Stanton as his secretary of war. This action violated a Tenure of Office Act passed by Congress in 1867 to limit the powers of the presidency. Stanton refused to give up the office, and the Senate supported him. The House then voted to impeach the president—the first such occurrence in U.S. history. In the subsequent Senate trial, the charges proved weak, and the necessary two-thirds vote needed for conviction failed by one vote. Johnson remained in office until 1869, but he had lost the ability to lead. He returned to Tennessee, where he won reelection to the Senate shortly before he died on July 31, 1875.

CHAPTER 14

HARRIET BEECHER STOWE

American writer and philanthropist Harriet Beecher Stowe was the author of the novel *Uncle Tom's Cabin*, which contributed so much to popular feeling against slavery that it is cited among the causes of the American Civil War.

Harriet Beecher was born on June 14, 1811, in Litchfield, Conn. Her father, Lyman Beecher, was a renowned preacher. Harriet was a student, and later a teacher, at Hartford Female Seminary. In 1832 the Beechers moved to Cincinnati, Ohio. Just across the Ohio River lay slave territory. Beecher's visits to plantations confirmed her disdain for slavery. In 1836 Beecher married Calvin Ellis Stowe, a seminary professor who encouraged her literary activity. She wrote continually and in 1843 published *The Mayflower; or, Sketches of Scenes and Characters Among the Descendants of the Pilgrims.* In 1850 her husband became professor at Bowdoin College and the family moved to Brunswick, Maine.

There Harriet Stowe began to write a long tale of slavery, based on her reading of abolitionist literature and on her personal observations. Her tale was published serially (1851–52) in the *National Era*, an antislavery paper of Washington, D.C.; in 1852 it appeared in book form as *Uncle Tom's Cabin; or, Life Among the Lowly.* The book was an immediate sensation and was taken up eagerly by abolitionists while, along with its author, it was vehemently denounced in the South, where reading or possessing the book became an extremely dangerous enterprise. With sales of 300,000 in the first year, the book exerted an influence equaled by few other novels in history, helping to solidify both pro- and antislavery sentiment. The book was translated widely and several times dramatized (the first time, in 1852, without Stowe's permission), where it played to capacity audiences. Stowe was enthusiastically received on a visit to England in 1853, and there she formed friendships with many leading literary figures. In that same year she published *A Key to Uncle Tom's Cabin*, a compilation of documents and testimonies in support of disputed details of her indictment of slavery.

A theater poster depicting a scene from a late 19th-century stage production of Uncle Tom's Cabin. *Pres. Abraham Lincoln and author Harriet Beecher Stowe are seen in the top corners.* Transcendental Graphics/Archive Photos/Getty Images

In 1856 she published *Dred: A Tale of the Great Dismal Swamp*, in which she depicted the deterioration of a society resting on a slave basis. She thereafter led the life of a woman of letters, writing novels, of which *The Minister's Wooing* (1859) is best known, many studies of social life in both fiction and essay, and a small volume of religious poems. Late in her life she assisted her son Charles E. Stowe on a biography of her, which appeared in 1889. She died in Hartford, Conn., on July 1, 1896.

CHAPTER 15

HORACE GREELEY

American newspaper editor and political leader Horace Greeley was the founder of the highly influential *New York Tribune*, a daily paper dedicated to reforms, economic progress, and the elevation of the masses. He was a great molder of public opinion in the period just before and during the Civil War.

Greeley was born on Feb. 3, 1811, in Amherst, N.H. He learned the printing trade in Vermont. In 1831 he went to New York City with $10 in his pocket and his clothes in a bundle carried over his shoulder. After several newspaper ventures he started the *New York Tribune* in 1841. He edited the paper for the rest of his life.

During the 1850s Greeley became known for his vigorous expression of the North's antislavery sentiments. At first he believed that the differences between the North and the South could be settled peacefully. Shortly before the Civil War, however, Greeley and his newspaper dropped their pacifist role. When the war began he disagreed with President Lincoln's conduct of it. He also urged the emancipation of the slaves before Lincoln was ready for the step.

After the war Greeley wanted the North to treat the South leniently. To set an example, he signed the bond by which Jefferson Davis, the former president of the Confederacy, was given his freedom. In 1872 Greeley was the presidential candidate of the Liberal Republicans and the Democrats against Ulysses S. Grant. He was badly defeated. In this campaign he ran against the Republican candidate despite the fact that he was one of the founders of the Republican party. Greeley died on Nov. 29, 1872, in New York City.

CHAPTER 16

WENDELL PHILLIPS

For nearly 50 years Wendell Phillips was one of the foremost abolitionists, reformers, and orators in the United States. Although he often faced ridicule and the threat of mob violence, his belief in abolition and basic human rights was greater than any desire for popularity and any fear of danger.

Phillips was born on Nov. 29, 1811, in Boston, Mass. His father, a prominent judge, was the city's first mayor. An excellent student, Phillips attended the Boston Latin School, Harvard College, and Harvard Law School. He first gained recognition in 1837 with a stirring speech he delivered in Boston's Faneuil Hall, condemning the murder in Illinois of the antislavery editor Elijah P. Lovejoy. He advocated the disunion of free states from slave states and welcomed the American Civil War. During the war Phillips criticized President Abraham

Wendell Phillips. Library of Congress, Washington, D.C.

Lincoln for delaying emancipation. Phillips also advocated temperance, better working conditions, heavier taxation of the rich, and women's rights, and he condemned the history of ill-treatment of Indians in the United States. In 1870 he ran unsuccessfully for governor of Massachusetts as the candidate of the Labor and Prohibition parties. He died in Boston on Feb. 2, 1884.

CHAPTER 17

STEPHEN A. DOUGLAS

The author of the Kansas-Nebraska Act of 1854 was Stephen A. Douglas, a United States senator from 1847 until his death. He also gained national fame from a series of debates with Abraham Lincoln.

Stephen Arnold Douglas was born on April 23, 1813, at Brandon, Vt. At 20 he moved to Illinois. There he practiced law and entered politics. In 1843 he became one of the youngest members of the House of Representatives.

Douglas' Kansas-Nebraska Act provided that the people in these territories should decide whether the territories would join the Union as slave or as free states. The act was opposed by the antislavery leaders. Among these was Abraham Lincoln. In 1858 Lincoln ran against Douglas for the senatorship from Illinois, basing his campaign on the Kansas-Nebraska issue. Douglas won the senatorship. In the debate at Freeport, Ill., however, he was led to declare that any territory could by "unfriendly legislation" exclude slavery. This statement antagonized the South.

When the national Democratic convention met in 1860, the Southern delegates bolted the party rather than support Douglas for president. At a separate convention they named John C. Breckinridge as their candidate. The Northern Democrats nominated Douglas as their candidate. The split in the party made the election of Lincoln, the Republican candidate, a foregone conclusion.

Douglas then devoted his energy to opposing secession and loyally pledged his support to Lincoln and the Union. This work was cut short by his death from typhoid fever on June 6, 1861, in Chicago.

CHAPTER 18

GEORGE G. MEADE

In June 1863 the Union faced its darkest days in the Civil War. The Confederate Army, led by General Robert E. Lee, had not lost a battle in two years and was now striking northward into Pennsylvania. The Northern people were panic-stricken. New leadership was needed. On June 28 President Abraham Lincoln appointed General George G. Meade commander of the Army of the Potomac, replacing General Joseph Hooker.

George Gordon Meade was born on Dec. 31, 1815, in Cádiz, Spain, the son of a United States naval agent. He won an appointment to West Point in 1831. He graduated in 1835 and was immediately ordered to Florida for service in the Seminole Wars. A year later he resigned from the Army to work as a surveyor. Meade was married in 1840 and returned to the Army in 1842 as a second lieutenant in the Topographical Engineers.

Meade served well in the Mexican War, and when the Civil War broke out he became a brigadier general of volunteers. A few days after his appointment on July 1, 1863, a surprise encounter plunged his army into the Battle of Gettysburg. Through three days of terrific fighting, Meade defended the Union position against all Confederate attacks. Lee finally acknowledged defeat by withdrawing to Virginia.

Meade was severely criticized at the time for failing to pursue and crush the shaken Confederates. Nonetheless, he had succeeded in defeating Lee and had broken the string of Confederate victories. In 1864 he received the thanks of Congress and was commissioned a major general in the regular army. He retained his command until the end of the war, but after General Ulysses S. Grant took over all Union forces in March 1864, Meade had only nominal leadership of the Army of the Potomac.

After the war Meade commanded the division of the Atlantic in 1865–66 and the department of the east in 1866–67. In 1868–69 he commanded the military district that included Georgia, Alabama, and Florida, where his firm justice helped ease the difficult period of Reconstruction. Meade died in Philadelphia, Pa., on Nov. 6, 1872.

CHAPTER 19

JUBAL A. EARLY

A Confederate general in the Civil War, Jubal A. Early commanded an army that at one time threatened Washington, D.C. His forces, however, suffered a series of defeats during the Shenandoah Valley campaigns of late 1864 and early 1865 that led to the final collapse of the South.

Jubal Anderson Early was born on Nov. 3, 1816, in Franklin County, Va. A West Point graduate, Early served in the Second Seminole War in Florida and the Mexican War. In the period leading up to the Civil War, he strongly opposed secession, but when Virginia decided to withdraw from the Union in 1861, he felt obliged to conform to the action of his state.

As an officer in the Confederate Army of Northern Virginia, Early rendered conspicuous service at the First Battle of Bull Run, near Manassas, Va., and served throughout the Virginia campaigns of 1862–63 and at Gettysburg (July 1863). The climax of his

Confederate Lt. Gen. Jubal A. Early. **Library of Congress Prints and Photographs Division**

career came in the summer of 1864 when General Robert E. Lee placed him in command of all Southern forces in the strategic Shenandoah Valley. His first action was to drive the Union forces under General David Hunter out of the state and to move down the valley unopposed. He then crossed the Potomac River, reaching Hagerstown and Frederick in Maryland, and defeated a small Union force at the Battle of Monocacy (July 9, 1864). Two days later he led 8,000 troops past Silver Spring and brought them into sight of Washington before withdrawing.

Northern pride was wounded by Early's threat, and General Ulysses S. Grant dispatched General Philip Sheridan to clear the valley once and for all. Bowing to numerically superior forces, Early suffered three decisive defeats at Sheridan's hands between September 19 and October 19—at Winchester, Fishers Hill, and Toms Brook—after which the valley was laid waste. Early then carried out a well-planned attack at Cedar Creek but was forced to retreat up the valley to Waynesboro, where he experienced the final defeat, on March 2, 1865, that ended Confederate resistance in that area and opened the way to Union capture of Richmond.

After the Confederate surrender in April 1865, Early went to Mexico and then Canada, where he published *A Memoir of the Last Years of the War of Independence in the Confederate States of America* (1866). In 1869 he returned to Virginia, where he practiced law and wrote historical essays. He died on March 2, 1894, in Lynchburg, Va.

CHAPTER 20

BENJAMIN F. BUTLER

During the Civil War, Benjamin F. Butler served as a major general in the Union Army. He was also a prominent politician of the era and played a leading role in the impeachment trial of President Andrew Johnson.

Benjamin Franklin Butler was born on Nov. 5, 1818, in Deerfield, N.H. He graduated from Colby College in Maine in 1838 and from 1840 practiced law in Massachusetts. In the 1850s he served two terms in the Massachusetts state legislature. He was appointed a Union officer after the Civil War broke out. As a brigadier general of the Massachusetts militia, Butler commanded the troops that occupied Baltimore, Md., and in May 1861 was promoted to the rank of major general in command of Fort Monroe in Virginia. There he refused to return fugitive slaves to the Confederacy, using the logic that they constituted "contraband of war"—an interpretation later upheld by his government. In June 1861 he lost the engagement at Big Bethel, Va., but succeeded in capturing the forts guarding the inlet at Hatteras, N.C., two months later.

Early in 1862 Butler was given command of the land forces that accompanied the victorious Union expedition against New Orleans. The city fell late in April, and from May to December Butler ruled it with an iron hand: he executed a citizen who had torn down the U.S. flag, undertook sanitary measures to prevent an outbreak of yellow fever, and confiscated the property of Confederate sympathizers. He was recalled at the end of the year.

As commander of the Army of the James in Virginia in 1864, Butler became bottled up in Bermuda Hundred, Va., and was unsuccessful in operations before Richmond and Petersburg. After the failure of an expedition against Fort Fisher in North Carolina, he was relieved of his command in January 1865.

After the war, Butler became a Radical Republican in the U.S. House of Representatives (1867–75, 1877–79), supporting firm Reconstruction measures toward the South and managing the impeachment trial of President Andrew Johnson. Although a staunch supporter of President Ulysses S. Grant after 1868, he broke with the party in 1878 because of his sympathy with the Greenback movement (a campaign to maintain or increase the amount of paper money in circulation). After two unsuccessful tries, Butler was elected Democratic governor of Massachusetts in 1882 and two years later became the presidential candidate of the Greenback-Labor party and the Anti-Monopoly party. He advocated the eight-hour day and national control of interstate commerce but failed to win a single electoral vote.

At various times in his career Butler was accused of corruption, but no charges against him were ever proved. He died on Jan. 11, 1893, in Washington, D.C.

CHAPTER 21

JULIA WARD HOWE

American author, social reformer, and lecturer Julia Ward Howe is best known for her "Battle Hymn of the Republic." During a visit to an army camp near Washington, D.C., in 1861, she wrote the poem, which was intended to be set to an old folk tune also used for "John Brown's Body." Published in February 1862 in the *Atlantic Monthly*, "Battle Hymn of the Republic" became the semiofficial Civil War song of the Union Army.

Julia Ward was born to a well-to-do family in New York, N.Y., on May 27, 1819. She was educated privately and in 1843 married educator Samuel Gridley Howe. Always of a literary bent, she published her first volume of poetry, *Passion Flowers*, in 1854; this and subsequent works—including a poetry collection, *Words for the Hour* (1857), a play, *Leonora; or, the World's Own*, produced in 1857, and *A Trip to Cuba* (1860)—had little success.

For a while Howe and her husband published the *Commonwealth*, an abolitionist newspaper. The publication of "Battle Hymn of the Republic" made Howe famous. After the war she involved herself in the woman suffrage movement. In 1868 she helped form and was elected the first president of the New England Woman Suffrage Association, an office she held until 1877, and from 1869 she took a leading role in the American Woman Suffrage Association. Howe also took up the cause of peace and in 1870 published her "Appeal to Womanhood Throughout the World," a call for an international conference of women on the subject of peace. In 1871 she became first president of the American branch of the Woman's International Peace Association.

Howe continued to write throughout her life, publishing travel books, poetry, collections of essays, and biographies. She founded a short-lived literary journal, *Northern Lights*, in 1867 and was a founder in 1870 and an editor for 20 years thereafter of the *Woman's Journal*. She was a frequent traveler until extreme old age. Howe was again president of the New England Woman Suffrage Association from 1893 to 1910. In 1908 she became the first woman to be elected to the American Academy of Arts and Letters. She died on Oct. 17, 1910, in Newport, R.I.

CHAPTER 22

WILLIAM TECUMSEH SHERMAN

Ranked second only to General Ulysses S. Grant as the greatest Northern commander in the Civil War, General William Tecumseh Sherman was a master of modern warfare. Like Grant, Sherman was born in Ohio when it was a frontier state. He was named Tecumseh for the Shawnee Indian chief who had defended that region against white settlement a few years earlier.

Sherman was born on Feb. 8, 1820, in Lancaster, Ohio. His father died when the boy was 9 years old. Most of the 11 children in the family were distributed among the relatives and friends. He was adopted by Thomas Ewing.

After attending an academy at Lancaster, Sherman entered West Point. During the Mexican War he saw service in California. In 1853 he resigned his commission for a business, legal, and educational career. When Louisiana seceded from the Union, he was head of the state military academy (now Louisiana State University). He resigned his position and rejoined the Army in May 1861.

William Tecumseh Sherman, photographed by Matthew Brady, c. *1860–1865.* National Archives, Washington, D.C.

He was commissioned a colonel of volunteers and commanded a brigade in the First Battle of Bull Run, on July 21, 1861. Three months later he was given charge of the Department of the Ohio (River). On taking over his new command he reported that 200,000 men would be needed to carry on a successful campaign in that region.

General William Tecumseh Sherman* (center) *poses with his staff.
National Archives, Brady Collection, Civil War Photographs

Newspapers said that Sherman was crazy. Time proved him right, but popular protest cost him his command.

Sherman's military genius was so outstanding that he could not long be kept in the background. He distinguished himself at the Battle of Shiloh (April 6–7, 1862) and won promotion to the rank of major general.

In the Vicksburg campaign Sherman rendered valuable aid to Grant. At its successful conclusion he generously gave all the credit to his superior officer. When Grant, as a result of this campaign, was made commander of the armies of the United States, Sherman was appointed to fill Grant's position as commander in the West.

It was in this position that Sherman undertook the campaign on which his fame chiefly rests. On May 6, 1864, he left Chattanooga, Tenn., for Atlanta, Ga. It took him four months to cover the 135 miles (215 kilometers) between the two places, for in this campaign he met a worthy foe in General Joseph E. Johnston, the Confederate commander. Sherman reached Atlanta on September 2. After clearing the city of its civil population and resting his troops, Sherman started on his famous "March to the Sea." For 32 days

General William Tecumseh Sherman (leaning on rear of gun cannon) talks with his staff at a Union fort in Atlanta, Ga., in 1864. Library of Congress, Washington, D.C.

no news of him reached the North. He had cut himself off from his base of supplies, and his troops lived on what they could get from the country through which they passed. They covered a path 60 miles (95 kilometers) wide in their march, and in that path they ruthlessly destroyed everything that they could not use but that might prove of use to the enemy. In view of this destruction, it is understandable that Sherman later declared that "war is hell." Finally, on December 20, Sherman reached Savannah, Ga., and telegraphed to President Lincoln: "I beg to present you as a Christmas gift the city of Savannah, with 150 heavy guns and plenty of ammunition, and also about 25,000 bales of cotton."

After a month's rest Sherman turned northward with his army, expecting to join Grant near Richmond, the Confederate capital. But before Sherman reached the area the Confederacy had collapsed. After receiving the surrender of General Johnston in North Carolina, Sherman marched on to Washington.

Sherman remained in the Army as commander in the West until Grant became president in 1869. Sherman then assumed command of the entire Army. He held that post until November 1883 and retired from active duty early in 1884. That year it was proposed that he run for president. His response was: "If nominated, I will not run. If elected, I will not serve." In 1886 he moved to New York City, where he died on Feb. 14, 1891.

CHAPTER 23

HARRIET TUBMAN

A runaway slave herself, Harriet Tubman helped so many blacks escape to freedom that she became known as the "Moses of her people." During the Civil War she served the Union Army as a nurse, cook, scout, and spy.

Harriet Tubman was born Araminta Ross about 1820 on a plantation near Bucktown, Md. She was one of 11 children of a slave couple. At 7 she was hired out to do housework and to care for white children on nearby farms. Later she became a field hand. While still a teenager, she was struck on the head by an overseer. As a result of the blow, she fell asleep suddenly several times a day for the rest of her life. Hard work toughened her, and before she was 19 she was as strong as the men with whom she worked.

In 1844 Ross married a free black, John Tubman. She left him in 1849, when her fear of being sold farther south spurred her to escape. She traveled at night, aided by the Underground Railroad, a secret network of people who helped fugitive slaves reach the Northern states and Canada.

Harriet Tubman. Library of Congress, Washington, D.C.

In Philadelphia, Pa., and later at Cape May, N.J., Tubman worked as a maid in hotels and clubs. By December 1850 she had saved enough money to make the first of 19 daring journeys back into the South to lead other slaves out of bondage. In 1851 she returned for her husband but found he had remarried.

Tubman worked closely with the Underground Railroad. Often she left fugitives in the care of other "conductors" after leading them part of the way herself. She maintained strict discipline during the perilous journeys to the North. If a runaway lagged behind or lost faith and wished to turn back, she forced him on at gunpoint. Before the Civil War she freed her parents and most of her brothers and sisters as well as hundreds of other slaves.

Slaveowners were constantly on the lookout for Tubman and offered large rewards for her capture, but they never succeeded in seizing her or any of the slaves she helped escape during her work for the Underground Railroad. Much later in life she proudly recalled: "I never ran my train off the track, and I never lost a passenger."

Tubman supported her parents and worked to raise money for her missions into the South. She spoke at abolitionist meetings and at women's rights assemblies, often concealing her name for protection from slave hunters. Her forceful leadership led the white abolitionist John Brown to refer to her admiringly as "General" Tubman. She helped Brown plan his October 1859 raid on the federal arsenal at Harpers Ferry (now in West Virgina), and promised that many of the slaves she had freed would join him. Only illness prevented her from fighting at Brown's side during the raid itself.

During the Civil War Tubman served the Union Army. She nursed and cooked for white soldiers, as well as for sick and starving blacks who sought protection behind Union lines. She acted as both a scout and a spy, often bravely leading Union raiding parties into Confederate territory. For this, Tubman won the respect of many grateful Union officers. But her efforts went unrewarded. She spent many decades trying to collect 1,800 dollars in back pay from the federal government, which refused to recognize her wartime services. When in 1899 she was finally granted a pension, it was given to her not for her own deeds but because she was the widow of Nelson Davis, a Civil War veteran whom she had married in 1869.

Tubman had settled in Auburn, N.Y., in 1857. After the Civil War she fed, sheltered, and nursed any blacks who came to her home for aid. After many years of effort, she was able to sponsor a home for needy blacks in Auburn, which was opened in 1908.

Scenes in the Life of Harriet Tubman, her first biography, published in 1869, was written by Sarah Hopkins Bradford. In subsequent editions the title was changed to *Harriet Tubman: the Moses of Her People*. Harriet Tubman died in Auburn on March 10, 1913, and was buried with military honors. A year later the city unveiled a tablet in her memory.

CHAPTER 24

JAMES LONGSTREET

One of the leading Confederate generals during the Civil War was James Longstreet. He was one of General Robert E. Lee's most trusted officers (Lee famously referred to Longstreet as "my old war horse") and served as Lee's second in command at the Battle of Gettysburg.

Longstreet was born on Jan. 8, 1821, in Edgefield District, S.C. A graduate of West Point, he resigned from the U.S. Army when his native state seceded from the Union in December 1860; he was made a brigadier general in the Confederate Army. He fought in the first and second battles of Bull Run (July 1861; August–September 1862); was a division commander in the Peninsular Campaign (March–July 1862); and at Antietam (September 1862) and Fredericksburg (November–December 1862) commanded what was soon called the I Corps in the Army of Northern Virginia.

By the time of the Battle of Gettysburg in July 1863, Longstreet had been promoted to lieutenant general. Longstreet's performance at Gettysburg has long been debated. His critics argue that his delay in attacking and his slowness in organizing the climactic "Pickett's Charge" (which was disastrously repulsed in what became a major turning point in the war) were responsible for the Confederate defeat. Others, however, place the blame on Lee, citing his inability to cope with unwilling officers. In September 1863 Longstreet directed the attack at Chickamauga that broke the Federal lines. He was severely wounded in the Wilderness Campaign. In November 1864, although with a paralyzed right arm, he resumed command of his corps. He surrendered with Lee at Appomattox.

After the war Longstreet was unpopular in the South, particularly among those who sought to portray the Confederate effort as a noble "lost cause." They blamed him for the loss at Gettysburg and were angered by his support of President Ulysses S. Grant and the Republican party. Longstreet went on to serve as U.S. minister to Turkey (1880–81) and commissioner of Pacific railways (1898–1904). His reminiscences, *From Manassas to Appomattox*, appeared in 1896. Longstreet died on Jan. 2, 1904, in Gainesville, Ga.

CHAPTER 25

NATHAN BEDFORD FORREST

Confederate general Nathan Bedford Forrest was often described as a "born military genius"; his rule of action, "Get there first with the most men," became one of the most often quoted statements of the war. A major blemish on his record, however, was the Massacre of Fort Pillow (April 12, 1864)—the slaughter by his soldiers of more than 300 blacks after the surrender of Fort Pillow, Tenn.

Forrest was born on July 13, 1821, near Chapel Hill, Tenn. At the outbreak of the war, he raised a cavalry unit and, as a lieutenant colonel, took part in the defense of Fort Donelson, Tenn., in February 1862. After fighting with distinction at the Battle of Shiloh, he was promoted to brigadier general.

In June 1864 Forrest decisively defeated a superior Union force at Brice's Cross Roads, Miss., and throughout the year he conducted successful raids in Mississippi,

Nathan Bedford Forrest. Universal Images Group/Getty Images

Tennessee, and Alabama. He took part in the Confederate Army of the West's last disastrous campaign of Nashville in December 1864 and by May 1865 had been forced to surrender his entire command.

After the war Forrest was active in the railroad business, and was a leading organizer and the first Grand Wizard of the original Ku Klux Klan, a secret society advocating white supremacy.

CHAPTER 26

CLARA BARTON

The founder of the American branch of the Red Cross was Clara Barton, a nurse who was sometimes called the "angel of the battlefield."

Barton was born on Dec. 25, 1821, in Oxford, Mass. She was educated at home and began teaching at age 15. She attended the Liberal Institute at Clinton, N.Y. (1850–51). In 1852 in Bordentown, N.J., she established a free school that soon became so large that the townsmen would no longer allow a woman to run it. Rather than subordinate herself to a male principal, Barton resigned. She was then employed by the U.S. Patent Office in Washington, D.C., from 1854 to 1857 and again in 1860.

At the outbreak of the American Civil War, Barton showed characteristic initiative in organizing facilities to recover soldiers' lost baggage and in securing medicine and supplies for men wounded in the First Battle of Bull Run. She gained permission to pass through the battle lines to

Clara Barton. Encyclopædia Britannica, Inc.

distribute supplies, search for the missing, and nurse the wounded. Barton carried on this work through the remainder of the Civil War, traveling with the army as far south as Charleston, S.C., in 1863. In June 1864 she was formally appointed superintendent of nurses for the Army of the James. In 1865, at the request of Pres. Abraham Lincoln, she set up a bureau of records to aid in the search for missing men.

While in Europe for her health, Barton studied the action of the Red Cross in the Franco-Prussian War. On her return home in 1872 she campaigned to organize a branch of the Red Cross in the United States. She succeeded in 1881. For 23 years she directed Red Cross work in every great disaster. She resigned in 1904. Barton died on April 12, 1912, in Glen Echo, Md.

CHAPTER 27

ULYSSES S. GRANT

Ulysses S. Grant led the Federal armies to victory in the Civil War. So great was his popularity that the people twice elected him to the presidency, though he was less successful as a president than as a general.

Early Life

Hiram Ulysses Grant was born on April 27, 1822, in Point Pleasant, Ohio, near Cincinnati. When he was 17, his father obtained for him an appointment to West Point. The academy mistakenly recorded his name as Ulysses S. Grant, and he eventually accepted the name. He was the finest horseman at the academy, and he was so good in mathematics that he hoped to teach the subject.

Upon graduation Grant was assigned to Jefferson Barracks, near St. Louis, Mo. From 1846 to 1848 he fought in almost every battle of the Mexican War. Grant came back from Mexico a brevet captain. He then married Julia Boggs Dent, with whom he had four children. In 1852 Grant's regiment was ordered to the Pacific coast. Homesick, he resigned from the Army in 1854.

Julia's father gave Grant 80 acres (30 hectares) to farm near St. Louis. After failing at farming, Grant turned to selling real estate in St. Louis. He failed again and walked the streets looking for something to do. Finally he joined his brothers in their leather business in Galena, Ill.

Civil War

When the Civil War broke out in April 1861, President Abraham Lincoln issued a call to arms. Within two weeks Grant was recruiting and drilling volunteers in Galena. He took his troops to the Illinois capital, Springfield, where the governor made him a clerk. In June 1861 Grant was made colonel of an unruly volunteer regiment, which he trained within a month. Then, before even engaging the enemy, he was appointed brigadier general.

In February 1862 Grant and his forces won the first major Union victory of the war, capturing Fort Donelson on the Cumberland River in Tennessee. While he was besieging this fort, the Confederate general asked for an armistice. Grant replied, "No terms except an unconditional and immediate surrender can be accepted. I propose to move immediately upon your works." The Confederates surrendered the fort with some 15,000 prisoners. Newspapers in the North were filled with praise of "Unconditional Surrender" Grant, and Lincoln named him a major general.

The objective of the Federal campaign in the West was to cut the Confederacy in two by winning the Mississippi Valley. The first major success came in the Battle of Shiloh in southern Tennessee. In two days of fighting—April 6 and 7, 1862—Grant pushed the Confederate forces back to Corinth in Mississippi.

Grant spent the rest of 1862 making plans to take Vicksburg, the great Confederate stronghold on the Mississippi River. Vicksburg was a brilliant operation and showed Grant at his best. The fort surrendered unconditionally on July 4, 1863. Five days later Port Hudson, the last Confederate post on the Mississippi, fell.

When Grant returned to Tennessee, he set out to relieve a Union Army penned up in Chattanooga. The Confederates occupied the heights of Lookout Mountain and Missionary Ridge, which controlled the approaches to the city. On November 24 and 25 Union troops stormed the heights, and the Confederates fled into Georgia. All Tennessee was now captured, and the power of the Confederacy west of the Alleghenies was effectively broken.

Meanwhile, the war in the East had been dragging. In March 1864 Lincoln, still looking for a general to match against Robert E. Lee, appointed Grant lieutenant general and gave him command of all the Union armies. While General William T. Sherman rampaged across Georgia, Grant attacked Lee's forces in Virginia. On April 9, 1865, Lee surrendered, bringing the war to an end. In 1866 Congress revived for Grant the rank of full general, a title not used since George Washington had held it.

Presidency

Grant had never been interested in politics and belonged to no political party. President Andrew Johnson hoped to put through Lincoln's lenient plan for Reconstruction—that is, for bringing the Southern states back into the Union. The Radical Republicans in Congress demanded a harsh policy. Johnson hoped to have Grant's support, but Grant

Scenes in the life of Ulysses S. Grant, from his West Point graduation in 1843 through the American Civil War to Robert E. Lee's surrender at Appomattox Court House in 1865. **Library of Congress Prints and Photographs Division**

quarreled with him and was won over by the Radicals.

In 1868 the Republican convention in Chicago unanimously nominated Grant for president, with Schuyler Colfax of Indiana for vice president. His Democratic opponent was Horatio Seymour, a former governor of New York. The campaign was fought over problems of Reconstruction. Although Grant's popular majority was small, he received 214 electoral votes against 80 for Seymour. At 46, Grant was the youngest man yet elected president.

Grave problems confronted the country as Grant took office. The war had brought poverty and desolation to the South. To the North it had brought prosperity. Speculation was rife, and there was widespread corruption in both political and business life.

In 1869 two speculators, Jay Gould and James Fisk, attempted to corner the market on gold and pressured Grant to keep the U.S. treasury from selling it. Foreign trade was almost stopped. On Black Friday, Sept. 24, 1869, the U.S. treasury, with Grant's approval, suddenly put up for sale 4 million dollars in gold. The price plunged, causing the ruin of many speculators.

In 1872 reformers in the Republican party set out to defeat Grant for reelection. They organized the Liberal Republican party, which joined with the Democrats in supporting Horace Greeley, founder of the *New York Tribune*, for the presidency. The regular Republicans, called Stalwarts, renominated Grant. Grant won easily.

Grant's popularity declined as evidence of serious political corruption came to light. The government had given money and land grants to the new railways in the West. In 1873 it was found that certain members of Congress had been bribed to vote in the interests of the Union Pacific Railroad. The bribes were in the form of stock in a railway construction company, the Crédit Mobilier. In 1874 the Whiskey Ring scandal was uncovered. The ring was a combination of distillers and tax officers who defrauded the treasury of the tax revenue on whiskey. Grant was not personally implicated in the scandals, but he gave appointments to unfit people and stood by them after they had been shown to be dishonest.

Later Years

Grant reluctantly announced that he would not be a candidate for a third term because he knew that the scandals of his administration had turned the voters against him. After leaving office in 1877, he toured Europe and Asia and then moved to New York City. Grant unwisely invested all his money in a brokerage firm co-owned by his son. When his son's partner defrauded the firm, it crashed and left Grant in poverty. To earn money, he turned to writing. His friend Mark Twain offered to publish his memoirs. Grant finished his book about a week before he died on July 23, 1885.

CHAPTER 28

HIRAM R. REVELS

During the Civil War, American clergyman and educator Hiram R. Revels helped organize African American volunteer regiments for the Union Army. After the war, he won election to the U.S. Senate, becoming the first African American elected to that body.

Hiram Rhoades Revels was born on Sept. 27, 1822, in Fayetteville, N.C. The son of free blacks, he traveled to Indiana and Illinois to receive the education that was denied him in the South. He was ordained a minister in the African Methodist Episcopal Church in 1845 and eventually settled in Baltimore, Md., where he served as a church pastor and principal of a school for blacks. Soon after the outbreak of the Civil War, he began his work in recruiting black soldiers for the North. In 1863 he joined the Federal forces to serve as a chaplain to a black regiment stationed in Mississippi.

When the war ended, Revels moved to Natchez, Miss., and was elected state senator in 1869. In 1870 he was elected to the U.S. Senate to fill the unexpired term of the former Confederate president, Jefferson Davis. Upon leaving the Senate, Revels was appointed president of Alcorn University (later Alcorn State University). He died on Jan. 16, 1901, in Aberdeen, Miss.

CHAPTER 29

MATHEW BRADY

A pioneer in 19th-century photography, Mathew Brady was best known for his portraits of politicians and for his photographs of the American Civil War. In his early 20s he began carrying out a plan to photograph as many distinguished Americans as he could.

Brady was born in about 1823 near Lake George, N.Y. Little is known of his background except that he received minimal schooling. Around 1840 the artist and inventor of the telegraph, Samuel F.B. Morse, taught Brady how to take daguerreotypes—photographs produced on silver plates. Brady opened his first studio in New York City in about 1844 and began winning awards for his skillful work.

Brady's remarkable collection of presidential portraits included all but one American president from John Quincy Adams, the sixth president, to William McKinley, the 25th. The only exception during the half century of Brady's career as a photographer was William Henry Harrison,

Mathew Brady, c. 1850. FPG/Archive Photos/Getty Images

who died a month after his inauguration. In 1851 Brady won a medal for a collection of 48 uncolored daguerreotypes shown at the Crystal Palace Exhibition in London. He switched to the wet-plate process of photography in 1855.

At the outbreak of the Civil War in 1861, Brady decided to make a complete record of the conflict. He hired a staff of 20 photographers, who covered every phase of the war; this project became the forerunner of 20th-century newsphoto services. Many of the photographers later worked in theFar West for the Union Pacific Railroad and acted as official photographers for government railroad surveys.

Two black soldiers in the Union Army are seen aiming their rifles in this Mathew Brady photograph. **Kean Collection/Archive Photos/ Getty Images**

Although Brady's main wartime activities were directing his cameramen from his Washington, D.C., office and supervising the operation of his studios, he personally photographed some battlefields. He was at the First Battle of Bull Run in 1861 and at the battles of Antietam in 1862 and Gettysburg in 1863, among others. He also took memorable photographs of Abraham Lincoln in the field and of Robert E. Lee soon after he had surrendered his army at Appomattox Court House in Virginia in 1865. Brady died on Jan. 15, 1896, in New York, N.Y.

(Brady's photograph of Lee, as well as one of William Tecumseh Sherman, can be found on pages 41 and 92 of this book, respectively.)

CHAPTER 30

MARY CHESNUT

Mary Chesnut's *A Diary from Dixie* presents an insightful view of Southern life and leadership during the American Civil War. Although not a day-by-day account, A Diary is regarded highly by historians for its perceptive views of Confederate military and political leaders and for its insight into Southern society during the Civil War.

Mary Boykin Miller was born on March 31, 1823, in Pleasant Hill, S.C. She was the daughter of a prominent politician and grew up in an atmosphere of public service. She attended private schools in Camden and Charleston. In 1840 she married James Chesnut, Jr., who later served as a U.S. senator from South Carolina until he resigned to take an important role in the secession movement and the Confederacy.

Her husband was a staff officer, an aide to General P.G.T. Beauregard, and commanding general of the South Carolina reserves. Chesnut accompanied him on his military missions during the Civil War and began recording her views and observations on

February 15, 1861. She closed her diary on August 2, 1865. After the war she reworked her manuscript many times in anticipation of publication. Chesnut died on Nov. 22, 1886, in Camden, but *A Diary from Dixie* was not published until 1905. An annotated edition with a biographical essay, *Mary Chesnut's Civil War*, edited by C. Vann Woodward, appeared in 1981 and was awarded the 1982 Pulitzer Prize in U.S. history.

CHAPTER 31

STONEWALL JACKSON

A Confederate general in the American Civil War, Stonewall Jackson was one of that conflict's most skillful tacticians. His military genius made him admired by friend and foe alike.

Thomas Jonathan Jackson was born on Jan. 21, 1824, in Clarksburg, Va. (now West Virginia). When Thomas was 3 years old his parents died penniless, and he went to live with his uncle.

After attending a small country school in Virginia, he decided to go to the United States Military Academy at West Point, N.Y. He set out for Washington, D.C., traveling part of the way on foot. When he arrived he presented himself before the secretary of war and asked for an appointment to the academy. The secretary, impressed by the boy's determination, immediately gave him the appointment.

After his graduation, in 1846, Jackson served in the Mexican War. In seven months he rose from second lieutenant to major. In 1851 he resigned from the army to teach at Virginia Military Institute.

He continued teaching until 1861, when the crisis arose between the North and the South. Jackson wanted to see the Union preserved, but he believed that the South had a just cause. He therefore supported it. His record won him a commission as colonel and rapid promotion to brigadier general.

General Barnard E. Bee is credited with giving Jackson his nickname. At the First Battle of Bull Run, Jackson's troops held firm when others wavered. Bee rallied his disorganized men with: "There is Jackson standing like a stone wall." Thereafter Jackson was known as Stonewall.

Stonewall Jackson marched his men swiftly and over long distances into battle. Stonewall Jackson's troops became known as "Jackson's foot cavalry." His strict discipline and long marches tested his men to the limits of their endurance, but they admired and loved their commander.

In May 1863 at Chancellorsville, Va., Jackson half-circled the Union Army and surprised it from behind. This attack contributed largely to the Confederate victory. But at dusk on May 2, as Jackson and his escort returned from an observation

This statue of Stonewall Jackson stands on the grounds of the state capitol in Charleston, West Virginia. Todd Taulman/Shutterstock.com

point, one of his own outposts mistook them for a detachment of Federal cavalry and fired. Jackson fell, seriously wounded, and died eight days later of pneumonia. Jackson is remembered as a great general and as an earnest and religious man. On the march he carried two books: Napoleon's *Maxims of War* and the Bible. He died on May 10, 1863, Guinea Station (now Guinea), Va.

CHAPTER 32

WINFIELD SCOTT HANCOCK

One of the best Union officers of the Civil War, Winfield Scott Hancock was a fearless and capable leader. Ulysses S. Grant said of him, "Hancock stands the most conspicuous figure of all who did not exercise a separate command."

Hancock was born on Feb. 14, 1824, in Montgomery County, Pa. He graduated from West Point in 1844 and fought in the Mexican War. A captain when the Civil War broke out, Hancock was soon commissioned brigadier general. He helped organize the Army of the Potomac, and in 1862 served in the battles of South Mountain and Antietam. At Fredericksburg, that December, he led a desperate attack on Marye's Height through a deadly fire. At Gettysburg in 1863, his appearance on Cemetery Ridge on the first day of the battle was equal to reinforcement by an army corps. Men who were fleeing stopped and the troops were restored to order.

Hancock commanded the Second Corps, and it was his forces that, on the last day of the battle, stopped the charge of General George Pickett's men, depriving the South of all hope of victory. Hancock was wounded, but he stayed on the field until victory was won. He recovered and in 1864 took part in the hard-fought battles of the Wilderness, Spotsylvania, and Cold Harbor. At Spotsylvania his troops broke through the Confederate defenses, capturing 3,000 prisoners. He was promoted to the rank of major general in 1866.

In 1880 the Democratic party nominated Hancock for the presidency. He lost the election to James A. Garfield. Hancock remained in the Army. He died on Feb. 9, 1886, on Governors Island, N.Y.

CHAPTER 33

GEORGE B. MCCLELLAN

An able administrator, a good organizer, and a popular leader, George B. McClellan had one flaw that ruined his career as a general. He was reluctant to fight.

George Brinton McClellan was born on Dec. 3, 1826, in Philadelphia and graduated from West Point in 1846. He was made a captain during the Mexican War, and in 1855 the U.S. government sent him to Europe to study the Crimean War.

At the beginning of the Civil War, in May 1861, President Abraham Lincoln appointed McClellan a major general in the U.S. Army. Immediately he was sent into western Virginia, where he rendered valuable assistance to the loyal Unionists who were seceding from Virginia to form what is now West Virginia. He was then called to Washington to reorganize the Army of the Potomac after its defeat at Bull Run. McClellan's aptitude for this work was soon apparent. In a short time order appeared where confusion had reigned. In November 1861 Lincoln appointed him commander of

A hand-colored Currier and Ives lithograph of George B. McClellan. Library of Congress Prints and Photographs Division

the U.S. Army. McClellan had built a wonderful military machine, but he hesitated to use it. Winter passed, and still he made no move against the enemy.

Finally in April 1862, under direct orders from the president, he entered upon his disastrous Peninsular Campaign between the York and James rivers of Virginia. He advanced within a few miles of Richmond. On July 1, after a terrible week of fighting known as the Seven Days' Battles, he was driven back and was directed to abandon the peninsula. A large part of his army was ordered to reinforce General John Pope's troops, and the order was reluctantly obeyed.

Pope's disastrous defeat in the Second Battle of Bull Run gave McClellan a new chance to retrieve his fame. Again in supreme command of the Army of the Potomac, he met Lee along Antietam Creek, Md., where on Sept. 17, 1862, there occurred one of the bloodiest battles of the war. Lee was forced to withdraw from Maryland, but McClellan, instead of driving forward at once, allowed Lee to recross the Potomac unmolested. In November McClellan was relieved of his command.

Lincoln was bitterly criticized for his action because McClellan still had many devoted admirers. In the election of 1864 all who were dissatisfied with Lincoln's conduct of the war supported McClellan for president, but he carried only three states—New Jersey, Kentucky, and Delaware. McClellan had resigned his commission in the Army before the election took place. The rest of his life he worked as an engineer, except from 1878 through 1881 when he was governor of New Jersey. He died in Orange, N.J., on Oct. 29, 1885.

CHAPTER 34

PHILIP SHERIDAN

Philip Sheridan ranks with Ulysses S. Grant and William T. Sherman as one of the three great Union commanders of the Civil War. Of the three he was the only one who devoted his whole life to the U.S. Army.

Sheridan was born in Albany, N.Y. His parents had settled there after emigrating from Ireland. Soon after his birth the family moved to Perry County, Ohio. The Mexican War prompted Sheridan to become a soldier. He secured an appointment to West Point, graduating from there in 1853.

Sheridan was a first lieutenant when the Civil War began. Distinguished service brought him rapid promotions. When Grant took command of the U.S. Army in 1864, he gave Sheridan command of the cavalry of the Army of the Potomac. During the Wilderness Campaign of 1864, Sheridan aided Grant by destroying Confederate lines of communication.

In July 1864 a strong Confederate force under Jubal Early drove the Federal Army from the Shenandoah Valley in northwestern Virginia. Sheridan was given command of the area. He defeated Early at Winchester and again at Fisher's Hill, driving the Confederates

Major General Philip Henry Sheridan and his generals, c. 1865. From left to right, Generals Wesley Merritt, Sheridan, George Crook, James William Forsyth, and George Armstrong Custer. Custer would go on to lead his men to death in battle against a group of Native Americans, one of the most controversial battles in U.S. history. **Library of Congress Prints and Photographs Division**

back to Staunton. These victories won for Sheridan a commission as brigadier general.

On the morning of October 19, Early counterattacked at Cedar Creek and drove the Federal force back in confusion. At that time Sheridan was returning from a conference in Washington D.C. Reaching Winchester, 20 miles (32 kilometers) away, he learned of the turn of events. Speedily he rode forward and reorganized the Union troops. At 3 pm his forces attacked and drove the Confederates 30 miles (48 kilometers) up the valley. For this Sheridan was made a major general and received the thanks of Congress.

In March 1865 Sheridan rejoined the Army of the Potomac. At Five Forks he entrapped and routed George Pickett's troops, causing the Confederates to abandon Petersburg. When General Robert E. Lee started to retreat, Sheridan's cavalry blocked the Confederate escape route at Appomattox Court House. This forced Lee to surrender.

After the war Sheridan was placed in command in the Southwest near the Mexican border. Later he headed the Department of Missouri, with headquarters in Chicago.

During the great Chicago fire of 1871, Sheridan's troops helped maintain order in the city.

In 1870 Sheridan served as the American military observer with the Prussian army in the Franco-Prussian War. In 1884 he succeeded Sherman as general in chief of the U.S. Army. He received the rank of general a few months before his death. Sheridan died on Aug. 5, 1888, in Nonquitt, Mass.

CHAPTER 35

PETROLEUM V. NASBY

Writing under the pen name Petroleum V. Nasby, humorist David Ross Locke had considerable influence on public issues during and after the Civil War. He was an ardent Unionist and foe of slavery who published barbed satiric attacks on the Southern position.

Locke was born on Sept. 20, 1833, in Binghamton, N.Y. From an early age he worked as a printer and journalist for newspapers in New York and Ohio. In 1861, as editor of the *Findlay (Ohio) Jeffersonian*, he published the first of many satiric letters purporting to be written by one Petroleum Vesuvius Nasby. For more than 20 years Locke contributed "Nasby Letters" to the *Toledo Blade*, which under his editorship gained national influence. Many of the letters appeared also in such books as *The Nasby Papers* (1864) and *The Diary of an Office Seeker* (1881). Locke died on Feb. 15, 1888, in Toledo.

Locke's chief weapon was a heavy irony. His character Nasby, a coarse and vicious Copperhead, argued illiterately for the Southern position. (Copperhead was the name given during the Civil War to a Northerner who sympathized with the Confederate cause.) Nasby's poor spelling and grammar, twisted logic, and chronic exaggeration and boasting delighted Northern readers, including President Abraham Lincoln, who occasionally read Nasby letters to his Cabinet.

CHAPTER 36

JEB STUART

In the Civil War, Major General James Ewell Brown Stuart was the South's most brilliant cavalry leader. His nickname, Jeb, came from the initials of his given names. Stuart's hard-riding troopers formed a screen between General Robert E. Lee's Confederate forces and the Union armies. Behind that screen Lee secretly moved his armies at will. Stuart also spied out movements of the Northern Army and kept Lee, his superior, well informed.

Stuart was born on Laurel Hill Plantation, in Patrick County, Va., on Feb. 6, 1833. He graduated from West Point and was an aide to Lee in the defeat of John Brown's raid on Harpers Ferry. When the Civil War broke out, he resigned his commission and joined the South.

The Confederates made Stuart a lieutenant colonel. In 1861 at the First Battle of Bull Run his cavalry protected the Southern left and drove forward in a charge that aided victory. In 1862, at the age of 29, Stuart became a major general. His raids were famous. In

Gen. Jeb Stuart's raid around Gen. George B. McClellan, June 1862.
Library of Congress Prints and Photographs Division

1862, with 1,200 troopers, he circled George B. McClellan's army before Richmond. The same year, with 1,800 men, Stuart drove north into Chambersburg, Pa. In 1863, when Stonewall Jackson was fatally wounded during the Battle of Chancellorsville, Stuart took over the command of his troops and gained a notable victory.

Stuart, outnumbered, was mortally wounded at Yellow Tavern when he and his troops sought to keep Philip Sheridan's cavalry from reaching Richmond. He died in Richmond on May 12, 1864. After his death Lee said of him: "He was my ideal of a soldier."

CHAPTER 37

JOHN WILKES BOOTH

John Wilkes Booth was a member of one of the United States' most distinguished acting families of the 19th century, but he is best known for having assassinated President Abraham Lincoln on April 14, 1865.

Booth was born on May 10, 1838, near Bel Air, Md. He was the 9th of 10 children born to the actor Junius Brutus Booth; he showed excellent theatrical potential early on but also exhibited an emotional instability and a driving egocentricity that made it difficult for him to accept his brother Edwin's rise to acclaim as the foremost actor of the day. In 1859 Booth joined a Shakespearean stock company in Richmond, Va. He was widely acclaimed on a tour of the Deep South in 1860 and remained in demand as an actor throughout the Civil War.

A vigorous supporter of the Southern cause, Booth was outspoken in his advocacy of slavery and his hatred of Lincoln. He served briefly under General Robert E. Lee. Shortly after the war ended Booth shot Lincoln at Ford's Theatre in Washington, D.C.

He escaped to Richard H. Garrett's barn, near Fredericksburg, Va., but was fatally shot on April 26 when soldiers and detectives set fire to the barn and surrounded it. Opinion has been divided as to whether Booth killed himself or was killed by a soldier's bullet despite an order not to fire.

Broadside advertising a $100,000 reward for the capture of John Surratt, John Wilkes Booth, and David Harold (a misspelling of Herold), suspected of conspiring in the assassination of U.S. Pres. Abraham Lincoln, 1865. **Library of Congress Rare Book and Special Collections Division**

CHAPTER 38

ROBERT SMALLS

Robert Smalls was an African American slave who became a naval hero for the Union in the Civil War. He went on to serve as a congressman from South Carolina during Reconstruction. Smalls was born on April

372 HARPER'S WEEKLY. [JUNE 14, 1862.

ROBERT SMALLS, CAPTAIN OF THE GUN-BOAT "PLANTER."

THE GUN-BOAT "PLANTER," RUN OUT OF CHARLESTON, S. C., BY ROBERT SMALLS, MAY, 1862.

THE STEAMER "PLANTER" AND HER CAPTOR.

WE publish herewith an engraving of the steamer *Planter*, lately run out of Charleston by her negro crew, and a portrait of her captain, ROBERT SMALLS—both from photographs sent us by our correspondent at Hilton Head. The following, from the *Herald* correspondence, will explain the transaction:

The following are the names of the black men who performed this gallant and perilous service: Robert Smalls, pilot; John Smalls and Alfred Gradine, engineers; Abraham Jackson, Gabriel Turno, William Morrison, Samuel Chisholm, Abraham Allston, and David Jones. They brought with them the wife and three children of the pilot, and the wife, child, and sister of the first engineer, John Smalls. The balance of the party were without families.

The *Planter* is a high-pressure, side-wheel steamer, one hundred and forty feet in length, and about fifty feet beam, and draws about five feet of water. She was built in Charleston, was formerly used as a cotton-boat, and is capable of carrying about 1400 bales. On the organization

by Captain Relay, of the Confederate navy—all the other employés of the vessel, excepting the first and second mates, being persons of color.

Robert Smalls, with whom I had a brief interview at General Benham's head-quarters this morning, is an intelligent negro, born in Charleston, and employed for many years as a pilot in and about that harbor. He entered upon his duties on board the *Planter* some six weeks since, and, as he told me, adopted the idea of running the vessel to sea from a joke which one of his companions perpetrated. He immediately cautioned the crew against alluding to the matter in any way on board the boat, but asked them, if they wanted to talk it up in sober earnest-

on the following morning for Fort Ripley, and to be absent from the city for some days. The families of the contrabands were notified and came stealthily on board. At about three o'clock the fires were lit under the boilers, and the vessel steamed quietly away down the harbor. The tide was against her, and Fort Sumter was not reached till broad daylight. However, the boat passed directly under its walls, giving the usual signal—two long pulls and a jerk at the whistle-cord—as she passed the sentinel.

Once out of range of the rebel guns the white flag was raised, and the *Planter* steamed directly for the blockading steamer *Augusta*. Captain Parrott, of the latter vessel,

***Article in Harper's Weekly, June 14, 1862, detailing the heroic naval exploits of gunboat captain Robert Smalls.* Library of Congress Prints and Photographs Division**

5, 1839, in Beaufort, S.C. In 1861, at the outbreak of the war, he was sent into service in the Confederate navy and assigned to a frigate in Charleston harbor. In May 1862, he daringly took the ship, which also carried a dozen other slaves and Smalls' family, and delivered it to the Union side, thereby gaining freedom for all aboard. This earned him a job in the Union navy, where he was the highest-ranking African American officer from 1863 to 1866.

After the war, Smalls served in the South Carolina House of Representatives from 1868 to 1870 and in the state Senate from 1870 to 1874. He also served three terms in the U.S. House of Representatives (1875–79, 1882–83, 1884–87). Smalls died on Feb. 23, 1915, in Beaufort.

CHAPTER 39

SARAH EDMONDS

One of the most intriguing stories of the Civil War is that of Sarah Edmonds, who, disguised as a man, served in the Union Army as a soldier and spy.

Edmonds was born Sarah Edmonson in December 1841, probably in York County in the Canadian province of New Brunswick. She received scant education as a child, and sometime in the 1850s she ran away from home. For a time she was an itinerant seller of Bibles, dressing as a man and using the name Frank Thompson. She gradually made her way west and by 1861 had established residence in Flint, Mich. Shortly after the outbreak of the Civil War, she enlisted—as Frank Thompson—in a volunteer infantry company in Flint that became Company F, 2nd Michigan Infantry. Her disguise was a complete success for nearly a year. She took part in the Battle of Blackburn's Ford, the First Battle of Bull Run, and the Peninsular Campaign of April–July 1862. At Fredericksburg, December 13, 1862, she was an aide to Colonel Orlando M. Poe. At

Sarah Edmonds, c. 1870s. **Fotosearch/Archive Photos/Getty Images**

least twice she undertook intelligence missions behind Confederate lines "disguised" as a woman. She accompanied the 2nd Michigan to Kentucky early in 1863 and, for reasons that are unclear, deserted in April.

Taking the name Sarah Edmonds, she worked as a nurse for the United States Christian Commission. In 1865 she published a popular fictional account of her experiences as *Nurse and Spy in the Union Army*. She married in 1867 and was eventually granted a veteran's pension by Congress. She died on Sept. 5, 1898, in La Porte, Texas.

CONCLUSION

More than 150 years have passed since Confederate forces opened fire on Fort Sumter on April 12, 1861, an action that marked the beginning of the American Civil War, yet in the eyes of many scholars today, the war remains the central event in the history of the United States. The savage four-year conflict that followed the Battle of Fort Sumter settled once and for all a long series of quarrels between the North and the South over the crucial issue of slavery and the related question of states' rights. The ultimate victory of the Federal forces established that no state could secede from the Union or even nullify a national law. The war also paved the way for the adoption of the 13th Amendment, which forbade the use of slave labor in the United States.

The cost of the war was staggering, however, both in terms of material destruction and the loss of human lives. The enormous casualties suffered on both sides during the war have not ceased to astound historians. About 1,556,000 soldiers are estimated to have served in the Federal armies, which suffered a total of 634,703 casualties (359,528 dead and 275,175 wounded). There were probably about 800,000 men serving in the Confederate forces, which sustained approximately 483,000 casualties (about 258,000 dead and perhaps 225,000 wounded).

After the war the United States faced an array of social, political, and economic problems arising from the readmission to the Union of the former Confederate states. To the great misfortune of the nation, President Abraham Lincoln served only six weeks of his second term. His assassination proved to be particularly tragic for the South, as the new president, Andrew Johnson, could not provide the leadership necessary for an orderly change from war to peace.

During and after the Reconstruction period that followed the Civil War, the status of the liberated slaves remained a source of conflict. By the end of the 19th century, a new racial system had been put into place in the South, resting on the disenfranchisement of African American voters and a rigid system of racial segregation. Just as the failure of the United States to rid itself of slavery paved the way for civil war, so its failure to solve the problems of Reconstruction led directly to the race problems of a later day.

GLOSSARY

armistice A pause in fighting brought about by agreement between the two sides.

arsenal A place for the manufacture or storage of arms.

Black Friday (Sept. 24, 1869), when plummeting gold prices set off a U.S. stock-market panic.

brevet A commission giving a military officer a higher rank without an increase in pay.

brigadier A military commissioned officer with a rank just below major general.

cadet A student military officer.

cavalry Troops mounted on horseback.

circuit riding In the United States, the act of traveling within a judicial district (or circuit) to facilitate the hearing of cases.

Compromise of 1850 To maintain balance between free and slave states, five compromise measures were called for: the admission of California as a free state, allowing New Mexico and Utah to become territories with the slavery question left open, settlement of the Texas–New Mexico boundary dispute, a stronger fugitive slave law, and the prohibition of the slave trade in the District of Columbia.

electoral college A body of electors, especially one that elects the president and vice president of the United States.

flatboat A boat with a flat bottom and square ends used on rivers for carrying freight.

Freedmen's Bureau (1865–72) U.S. agency established during Reconstruction to help freed slaves in their transition to freedom.

homestead A tract of land acquired from United States public lands by filing a record and living on and cultivating the tract.

Know-Nothing party Formed in New York City in 1849 from the anti-immigrant and anti–Roman Catholic movement, this political party called for restrictions on both immigration and naturalized citizenship.

midshipman A student naval officer.

militia A body of citizens with some military training who are called to active duty only in an emergency.

mortar boat A boat adapted to carrying a mortar or mortars for bombarding.

nullify To make null or valueless; especially to make legally null and void.

posthumous Following or occurring after one's death, as in a posthumous award.

Radical Republican During and after the American Civil War, a member of the Republican party committed to emancipation of the slaves and later to the equal treatment and enfranchisement of the freed blacks.

Reconstruction The reorganization and reestablishment of the seceded states in the Union during a period (1865–1877) following the American Civil War.

statesman A person engaged in fixing the policies and conducting the affairs of a government; especially one having unusual wisdom and skill in such matters.

suffrage The right to vote. It is from the Latin word *suffragium*, which has several meanings, including "vote," "ballot," and "voting rights." Suffrage—also called franchise—is a civil right enjoyed by citizens of a democratic state.

tanner A person who tans hides, that is, changing hide into leather (by soaking hides in a tannin solution).

temperance The use of little or no alcoholic drink.

treason The offense of attempting to overthrow the government.

Whig A member of an American political party formed about 1834 in opposition to President Andrew Jackson and the Democrats. The Whig party was associated chiefly with manufacturing, commercial, and financial interests, and was succeeded in about 1854 by the Republican party. The name "Whig" was borrowed from the British party opposed to royal power or privilege.

FOR MORE INFORMATION

African American Civil War Museum
1925 Vermont Avenue, NW
Washington, DC 20001
(202) 667-2667
Web site: http://www.afroamcivilwar.org
The African American Civil War Museum honors the contributions and sacrifices made by African Americans during the Civil War. Artifacts, photographs, and more help tell the stories of these remarkable individuals.

American Historical Association (AHA)
400 A Street SE
Washington, DC 20003
(202) 544-2422
Web site: http://www.historians.org
The AHA serves as a leader and advocate for professionals, researchers, and students in the field of history and upholds academic and professional standards. The AHA also awards a number of fellowships and prizes and offers important resources and publications for anyone interested in the field.

The National Civil War Museum
One Lincoln Circle at Reservoir Park
Harrisburg, PA 17103

(717) 260-1861
Web site:
http://www.nationalcivilwarmuseum.org
The National Civil War Museum is committed to preserving artifacts, documents, photographs, and more from the Civil War era and presenting an unbiased view of the conflict to all visitors through its various exhibits.

National Museum of American History (NMAH)
14th Street and Constitution Avenue NW
Washington, DC 20002
(202) 633-1000
Web site: http://americanhistory.si.edu
With over three million artifacts of American history in its collection, many of which are on display, the NMAH is dedicated to promoting public interest in the events and individuals that shaped the American nation.

Organization of American Historians (OAH)
112 North Bryan Avenue
Bloomington, IN 47408
(812) 855-7311
Web site: http://www.oah.org

Committed to advancing scholarship in the field of American history, the OAH supports a number of programs, publications, and resources for students, teachers, researchers, and professionals in the field.

Web Sites

Due to the changing nature of Internet links, Rosen Educational Services has developed an online list of Web sites related to the subject of this book. This site is updated regularly. Please use this link to access the list:

www.rosenlinks.com/ioacb/civwarbio

FOR FURTHER READING

Brooks, Victor. *African Americans in the Civil War* (Chelsea House, 2000).

Clinton, Catherine. *The Civil War: An Illustrated History* (Scholastic, 1999).

Currie, Stephen. *Women of the Civil War* (Lucent Books, 2003).

Damon, Duane. *Growing Up in the Civil War, 1861 to 1865* (Lerner Publications, 2003).

Harmon, Daniel E. *Civil War Generals* (Chelsea House, 1998).

Marrin, Albert. *Commander in Chief Abraham Lincoln and the Civil War* (Dutton Children's Books, 1997).

McKissack, Pat, and McKissack, Fredrick. *Days of Jubilee: The End of Slavery in the United States* (Scholastic, 2003).

McPherson, James M. *Fields of Fury: The American Civil War* (Atheneum Books for Young Readers, 2002).

Ruggiero, Adriane. *Reconstruction* (Marshall Cavendish Benchmark, 2007).

Stanchak, John E. *Civil War* (Dorling Kindersley, 2000).

INDEX

A

abolitionists, 30, 33, 34, 36, 37, 42, 58, 70, 75, 89, 100
American Academy of Arts and Letters, 90
American Woman Suffrage Association, 90
Antietam, Battle of, 43, 102, 123, 130, 134
Anti-Monopoly party, 88
"Appeal to Womanhood Throughout the World," 90
Appomattox, 44, 103, 123, 138

B

Barton, Clara, 107–109
"Battle Hymn of the Republic," 89
Beauregard, P.G.T., 124
Bee, Barnard E., 127
Beecher, Lyman, 69
Black Friday, 115
Black Hawk War, 48, 56
Booth, Edwin, 145
Booth, John Wilkes, 63, 145–146
Booth, Junius Brutus, 145
Bradford, Sarah Hopkins, 101
Brady, Mathew, 120–123
Breckinridge, John C., 22, 23, 24, 59, 79
Brown, John, 33–37, 42, 100, 142
Buchanan, James, 16, 20, 21–25, 27
Bull Run, battles of, 42, 45, 82, 93, 102, 107, 109, 123, 127, 132, 134, 142, 149
Burnside, Ambrose E., 43
Butler, Benjamin F., 86–88

C

Chesnut, James, Jr., 124
Chesnut, Mary, 124–125
Clay, Henry, 14, 15
Colfax, Schuyler, 115
Commonwealth, 89
Compromise of 1850, 12, 15, 17, 28
Copperheads, 141
Custis, Mary, 40

D

Davis, Jefferson, 42, 45, 46, 48–52, 74, 119
Davis, Joseph, 48
Davis, Nelson, 101
Day, Mary Anne, 33

Dent, Julia Boggs, 110, 111
Diary from Dixie, A, 124, 125
Diary of an Office Seeker, The, 140
Douglas, Stephen A., 24, 58, 59, 78–79
Douglass, Frederick, 36
Dred, 72

E

Early, Jubal A., 82–85, 136, 137
Edmonds, Sarah, 149–150
Emancipation Proclamation, 60
Emerson, John, 26, 27
Everett, Edward, 61, 62
Ewing, Thomas, 91

F

Farragut, David, 38–39
Fillmore, Millard, 12–16, 22, 23
Fisk, James, 115
Ford's Theatre, 62–63, 145
Forrest, Nathan Bedford, 104–106
Fort Pillow, Massacre of, 104
Fourteenth Amendment, 29, 67
Franco-Prussian War, 109, 139
Freedmen's Bureau, 67
Free-Soilers, 23
Frémont, John C., 16, 22, 23

G

Garfield, James A., 131
Garrett, Richard H., 146
Gettysburg, Battle of, 43, 60, 81, 82, 102–103, 123, 130
Gettysburg Address, 61–62
Gould, Jay, 115
Grant, Ulysses S., 44, 60, 74, 81, 84, 87, 91, 94, 96, 103, 110–117, 130, 136
Greeley, Horace, 73–74, 116
Greenback-Labor Party, 88
Greenback movement, 88

H

Hamlin, Hannibal, 59
Hancock, Winfield Scott, 130–131
Harpers Ferry, 36, 37, 42, 100, 142
Harriet Tubman, 101
Hooker, Joseph, 80
Howe, Julia Ward, 89–90
Howe, Samuel Gridley, 89
Hunter, David, 84

J

Jackson, Andrew, 14, 15, 19, 64–68
Jackson, Stonewall, 126–129, 144
Johnson, Andrew, 16, 28, 29, 62, 63, 86, 87, 113, 115, 152
Johnston, Joseph E., 45–47, 94, 96
Johnston, Sarah Bush, 55

K

Kansas-Nebraska Act, 19–20, 78
Key to Uncle Tom's Cabin, A, 70
King, William R., 19
Know Nothings, 16, 22
Ku Klux Klan, 106

L

Lecompton Constitution, 23
Lee, Light-Horse Harry, 40
Lee, Robert E., 36, 40–44, 45, 51, 62, 80, 84, 102, 103, 113, 123, 134, 138, 142, 144, 145
Leonora, 89
Lincoln, Abraham, 15, 16, 21, 24, 25, 48, 50, 51, 53–63, 64, 65, 67, 73, 74, 75, 78, 79, 80, 96, 109, 111, 112, 113, 123, 132, 134, 135, 141, 145, 152
Lincoln, Nancy Hanks, 53
Lincoln, Thomas, 53
Locke, David Ross, 140–141
Longstreet, James, 102–103
Lovejoy, Elijah P., 75
Lusk, Dianthe, 33

M

"March to the Sea," 94–96
"Mary Chesnut's Civil War," 125
Mayflower, The, 69
McClellan, George B., 16, 42–43, 132–135, 144
McIntosh, Caroline Carmichael, 16
Meade, George G., 80–81
Memoir of the Last Years of the War of Independence in the Confederate States of America, A, 85
Mexican War, 15, 19, 40, 42, 48, 50, 80, 91, 110, 126, 130, 132, 136
Minister's Wooing, The, 72
Missouri Compromise, 26, 27
Morse, Samuel F.B., 120

N

Narrative of Sojourner Truth, The, 32
Nasby, Petroleum V., 140–141
Nasby Papers, The, 140
National Era, 70
New England Woman Suffrage Association, 90
New York Tribune, 73, 116
Northern Lights, 90

P

Passion Flowers, 89
Pemberton, John C., 46
Phillips, Wendell, 75–77
Pickett, George, 131, 138
"Pickett's Charge," 103
Pierce, Benjamin, 17
Pierce, Franklin, 15, 17–20, 22, 50
Pierson, Elijah, 30
Poe, Orlando M., 149
Polk, James Knox, 22
Pope, John, 134
Porter, David, 38
Powers, Abigail, 14, 16

R

Radical Republicans, 28, 64, 68, 87, 113, 115
Reconstruction, 16, 28, 64, 68, 81, 87, 113, 115, 147, 152
Red Cross, 107, 109
Revels, Hiram R., 118–119
Rise and Fall of the Confederate Government, The, 52
Robinson, Harriet, 26, 27

S

Scenes in the Life of Harriet Tubman, 101
Scott, Dred, 23, 26–27
Scott, Winfield, 15, 19, 40
Seminole Wars, 80, 82
Seven Days' Battles, 42, 134
Seymour, Horatio, 115
Sheridan, Philip, 84, 136–139, 144
Sherman, William T., 46, 91–96, 113, 123, 136, 139
Shiloh, Battle of, 94, 104, 112
Smalls, Robert, 147–148
Stalwarts, 116
Stanton, Edwin M., 68
Stevens, Thaddeus, 28–29
Stowe, Calvin Ellis, 69

Stowe, Charles E., 72
Stowe, Harriet Beecher, 69–72
Stuart, Jeb, 142–144
suffrage, 29, 90
Sumter, Fort, 24, 151

T

Taney, Roger B., 27
Taylor, Zachary, 12, 14
Tenure of Office Act, 68
Thirteenth Amendment, 62, 151
Todd, Mary, 56, 62
Trip to Cuba, A, 89
Truth, Sojourner, 30–32
Tubman, Harriet, 97–101
Tubman, John, 97
Twain, Mark, 117

U

Uncle Tom's Cabin, 69, 70
Underground Railroad, 34, 97, 99
Union Pacific Railroad, 116, 122

V

Vicksburg, 39, 46, 94, 112

W

Washington, George, 40
Washington, Martha, 40
Webster, Daniel, 14–15
Whigs, 12, 14, 15, 16, 19, 22, 28, 56
Whiskey Ring scandal, 116
Woman's International Peace Association, 90
Woman's Journal, 90
women's rights, 77, 100
Woodward, C. Vann, 125
Words for the Hour, 89